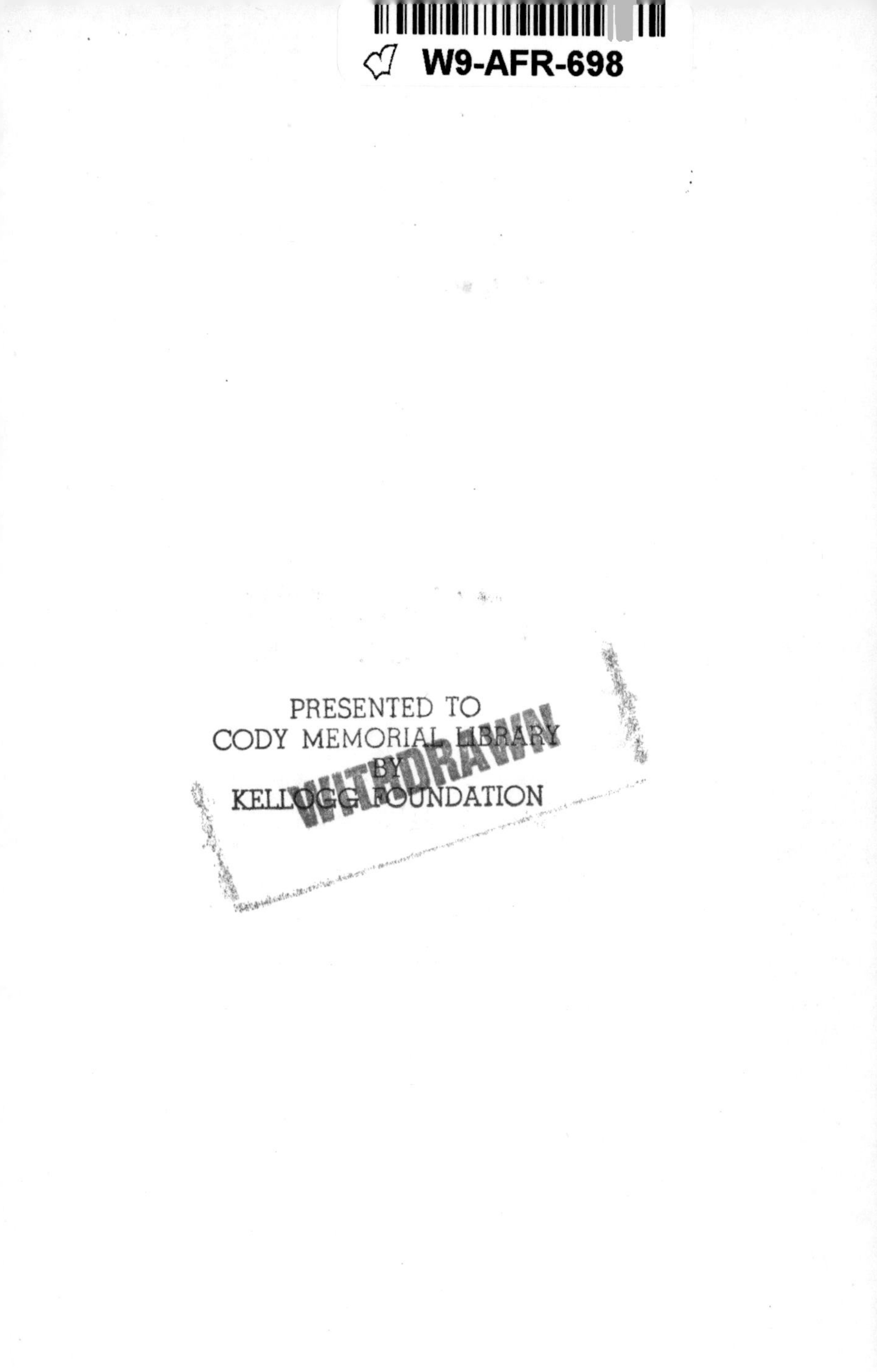
W9-AFR-698

PRESENTED TO
CODY MEMORIAL LIBRARY
BY
KELLOGG FOUNDATION

WITHDRAWN

# MESOPOTAMIA,
# THE CIVILIZATION THAT ROSE OUT OF CLAY

WALTER A. FAIRSERVIS, JR.

*Director of the Thomas Burke Memorial Washington State Museum of the University of Washington*

*Illustrated with photographs, and with drawings and maps by*
JAN FAIRSERVIS

THE MACMILLAN COMPANY, NEW YORK
COLLIER-MACMILLAN LIMITED, LONDON

# MESOPOTAMIA, THE CIVILIZATION THAT ROSE OUT OF CLAY

79985

Cody Memorial Library
Southwestern University
Georgetown, Texas

Titlepage illustration courtesy The Mansell Collection, London

Copyright © Walter A. Fairservis, Jr., 1964

*All rights reserved—no part of this book may be reproduced in any form without permission in writing from the publisher, except by a reviewer who wishes to quote brief passages in connection with a review written for inclusion in magazine or newspaper.*

LIBRARY OF CONGRESS CATALOG CARD NUMBER: 63–16103
PRINTED IN THE UNITED STATES OF AMERICA
*Designed by Andrew P. Zutis*

The Macmillan Company, New York
Collier-Macmillan Canada, Ltd., Toronto, Ontario

C
913.5
F167m

# CONTENTS

## SOME KINGS OF SUMER, AKKAD, AND BABYLONIA

## THE ASSYRIANS

## THE CHALDEAN BABYLONIANS

# ILLUSTRATIONS

*Photographs*

## *Drawings*

# INTRODUCTION

## THE ORIGIN OF CIVILIZATION

Man has lived on the earth perhaps some half million years. Throughout most of that immense span of centuries, man lived as a child in nature. His home was a cave or a hollow under a stone; his clothes were animal skins; his society was composed of a few individuals; his life was largely devoted to the hunting of animals with crude weapons. His path led over the earth from the far south of Africa to the north, west, and east of the Old World as far as the land extended.

In time, man gained knowledge from his experience as a hunter, and his ways changed. Techniques of toolmaking, ingenious devices for trapping animals, concepts of divinity, familiarity with the ways of nature were passed on from father to son. Given a land rich in deer, goat, buffalo, mammoth, and fish, lush with nuts, fruits, and nutritious plants, man learned to exploit these resources so expertly that he found time to do other things. Such a land was the Dordogne region of France, where are found to this day the cave paintings of artists dead more than twelve thousand years. Such a land also was the foothill country which rings the alluvial plains of Mesopotamia and Palestine in southwest Asia. The foothills were the native homes of wild cereals, wild goats, and sheep. Here early man found the hunting good and early woman the collection of herbs, nuts, and cereal kernels excellent.

In those far days, men knew nature in a way beyond

our comprehension. They might give a god's name to the thunder and the rain, and shudder with superstitious dread at the onset of a storm, but they well knew that the moist earth would provide things essential to their life and that these were not found in the hot plains of the Mesopotamian rivers, Tigris and Euphrates, or in the barren mountains whose heights rose beyond the foothills to climax in the snowy Caucasus.

They came to know the habits of the hoofed beasts of the hills, such as the wild goats that flocked while feeding and fled foolishly at one man's approach into the trap set by another. In such circumstances, a tiny kid left behind in the haste of its mother's frightened escape bleated its way into the hands of a man and grew to become accustomed to that man, who fed and fondled it—a goat that now never raced away at the man's approach but waited docilely for the shepherd it knew. From such experiences grew knowledge, and from one tame goat many. No longer did man need to follow the paths of the hills in endless search for game, for here in primitive domestication was a security unknown before. Added to this was a growing awareness of the miracle which each year creates the same plants in the same soil—plants which provide the wheat, barley, and millet kernels which birds, beasts, and man can devour, each in his own way. For man this awareness became knowledge; and what nature had planted haphazardly in her own way, man sowed in places which knowledge and experience taught him were best.

Domestication and agriculture were born out of man's intimacy with nature. Time which once was measured by good days to hunt and bad days of want was now bounded by a calendar of seasons. Months to sow, months to cultivate, months to reap; days of drought, days of plenty, days of hard work tilling the fields, days of rest awaiting harvest. The men of the fields were settlers on the good earth. But in the foothill country the good earth was limited. Men had to share the soil and the grass. This sharing drew them together, and out of a shared settled life grew the village. The village was the first center where a man's house and family could be found near a neighbor's house and family, and his to his neighbor's, and so on and on until at last there was a community that called itself a name and by that name was recognized by other villages.

The village became the center of life, the place where utensils were made and improved, where such things as containers evolved from gourds to wooden bowls to pottery, where robes gave place to fiber dress and thus to spun linen. The skilled craftsman, he who could work wood, bone, shell, and stone into pins, figures, daggers, beads, and tools, was the first to leave the fields for a shop at home. His food was supplied gladly by each farmer in exchange for a tool or an ornament. Then the medicine man, who by ritual perceived the gods' will in the ways of the world, became the priest, whose shrine, erected by all who lived in the village, was the hub about which all life moved.

Populations grew; fields were extended; new lands were sought; villages rose, from the Black Sea to the gates of the Nile. For thousands of years, thousands of farmers tilled the soil and fought, by prayer and sacrifice, with hoe and staff, to make the fields richer each year. They learned what seeds gave better crops, learned of the necessity for sufficient water, of the secrets of proper cultivation, and of the need to plant and harvest at certain times. Life grew complex—potters, priests, children, and wives needed food to thrive. But in the high country of the hills the number of fields was limited, and their fertility perhaps had decreased with constant use. The search for good land went on.

The mountains were not the place for farmers. But the land of the rivers was. Slowly, over perhaps a thousand years, the farmers of the hills in western Asia moved into the valley of the Tigris and Euphrates rivers—that land we now call Mesopotamia, where rules, the latest of many nations, the country called Iraq.

Mesopotamia means "in the midst of rivers." The rivers come from the hill country of the north and wander in mud-laden majesty across a flat plain, for all the world like two brown snakes winding sinuously toward the same goal —the waters of the Persian Gulf. The flat plain was actually created by the two rivers, for a large part of the silt torn from the slopes of the far mountains and carried to the plain becomes too heavy for the slow rivers and settles in the beds of the streams. There the silt remains submerged until the river course is changed as the water seeks a less-elevated bed. The silt then becomes hard-packed and dusty under the hot sun—hostile to life. But given rain, the dust subsides, and the soft mud swells with growing things.

To this land of hard, dusty earth and wandering rivers with banks of mud came the descendants of the farmers of the hills. Like ants crawling in an endless line on a chosen path from nest to food and back, men moved along the shores of the rivers. The shores were the muddy incubators which produced rich crops. As long as men were few, these shores were sufficient. It is probable that those early farmers who ventured to the south country wandered but little from the security of the river shores to cross the flat plain that stretched endlessly on all sides, barren and dusty much of the year. Yet there were times after rain when grass grew and herds could wander and fatten wonderfully. Those were the times when hillmen from the plateau of Persia, now Iran, or desert dwellers from Arabia in the south came to the valley of the two rivers—the hillmen with obsidian, copper, and ivory to trade; the desert people with hides, hair, and dyes.

But the farmers of the river banks were stopped at the great marsh where the rivers mingle before the sea of the Persian Gulf. But not for long. As life grew more complex, pressures arose to find new village sites, to control society with laws and rituals, to develop common understanding by using signs and symbols intelligible to all, to find new ways of doing things. These pressures were part of life on the flat plain of Mesopotamia. Before these pressures, even the marshes gave way. Farmers floored clay banks and shallow pools with layers of rushes, drained the swamps, shoveled the mud, and made the great marsh into solid land—a land which became the richest of the rich land of Mesopotamia. This was called the plain of Shinar, the land of the Sumerians, after the language of the black-haired farmers who settled there. The Sumerians were among the hardest-working farmers in history. They took the final steps which had been indicated six or seven thousand years earlier, when the hunters of the hills evolved domestication and agriculture. And those steps led to civilization.

Civilization means city or city-oriented culture. The Sumerian city was the village grown beyond itself. It is no coincidence that archaeologists digging deep under Sumerian cities find at last small villages in which, to the perceptive eye, the prophecy of a civilization to be created out of the mud of Mesopotamia is written in early artifacts.

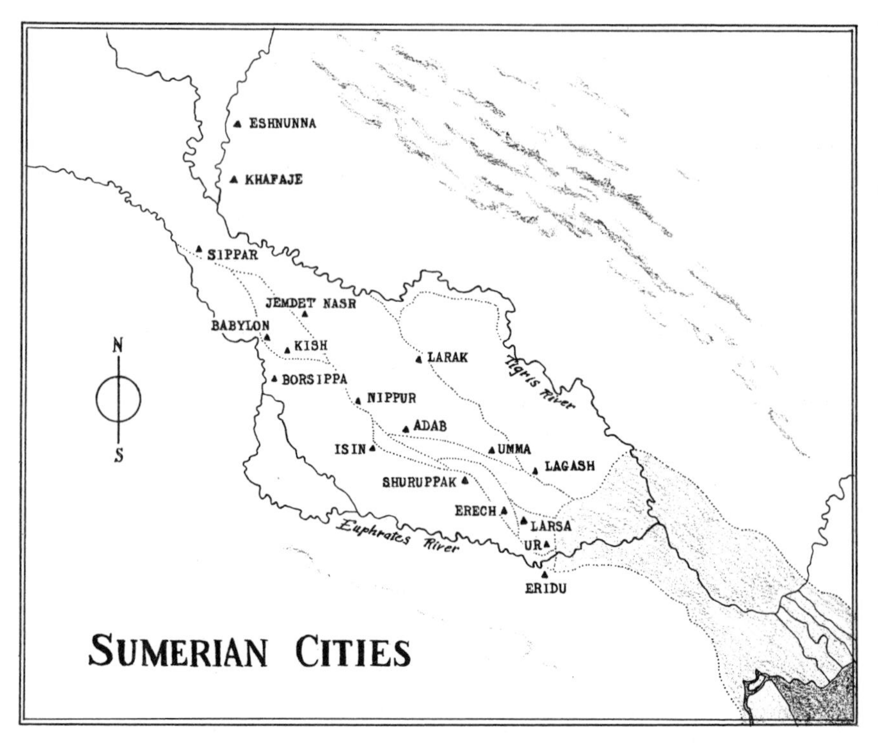


MAP OF SUMERIAN CITIES.

Sumerian civilization exists today in the world, for the civilization of the West owes many of its origins to the events that began around 3000 B.C. Writing, numbers, wheeled vehicles, architecture, industrialization, law—many things were formulated in Sumer. Later these things were to evolve elsewhere, and the Sumerians were to pass into history, the first in a long line of peoples and cultures until our times. Akkadians, Kassites, Assyrians, Chaldeans, Persians, Greeks, Romans, Turks, and Arabs at one time or another ruled Mesopotamia, each group in its own way. But each owed something to the others. Thus in the sum of the teeming story of Mesopotamia it is the Sumerians, and their civilization created out of the mud plain of two rivers, that made possible what came after.

The history of Mesopotamia extends over five millenniums, beginning around 3000 B.C. with Sumeria and today represented by Iraq. This history is a turbulent one, for the flat plains provided little protection from the invaders who came from the mountains to the north or from the deserts to the south and west. Kingdoms rose and kingdoms fell; empires blossomed and decayed. Much blood has been shed on the mud of Mesopotamia. But many things of benefit to man have been won on that same mud.

It is the early part of the story of Mesopotamia that interests us here, the ancient past that begins with the Sumerians, tells of the later Akkadians, Amorites, Kassites, and Assyrians, and ends in 539 B.C. with the fall of King Nebuchadnezzar's Babylon, celebrated in the Old Testament.

Briefly told, the first part of that history is this:

On the plain of Shinar (Sumeria), the Sumerians, who spoke a non-Semitic language, established little city-states, each with its patron deity or deities and its own traditions. Using extensive irrigation as the means of making the land prosper, the Sumerians developed a complex urban life in which writing, trade, and the advancement of technology had a leading part. The political structure consisted of a king with priestly powers and his advisers, who apparently represented the people, most of whom were farmers or craftsmen. (The important kings of the various dynasties are listed in the Appendix.) The various city-states (for example, Ur, Lagash, Kish, Eridu, Larsa, and Erech) were in constant conflict, and the accounts of the time give us many details of the rise and fall of power of these states.

Around 2100 B.C. the Akkadians, a Semitic-language-speaking group probably from Syria or Assyria in western Asia who had been settling around the city of Babylon, revolted against their Sumerian overlords and established an Akkadian kingdom, which consisted of the plain of Shinar and many lands bordering it. Sargon, an Akkadian general, led the revolt and became king. After a short but fruitful rule of less than one hundred years, the Akkadian period ended with a revolt by the Sumerians.

For a while there was prosperous Sumerian control under what came to be known as the Third Dynasty of Ur, but this too was short-lived. The quarrels between cities caused the breakup of central control, and Sumeria was the prey of invading forces—Amorites from the Syrian desert to the west and Elamites from Persia to the east. This was the true end of Sumerian political control. But Sumerian civilization was a legacy which the Amorites gladly accepted and incorporated into their own. Establishing their capital at Babylon around 1850 B.C., they founded the First Dynasty of Babylon. Their seventh king, Hammurabi is remembered today as the codifier of the laws of his time.

After Hammurabi's time, the Amorite control gradually succumbed to internal struggle and external invasion. Around 1550 B.C. the Kassites, a people who spoke an Indo-European language, moved down from the highlands of Persia in southwestern Asia and conquered the plain. We have very little information about their rule. For almost four hundred years the Kassites ruled not only on the plain but also in Assyria in western Asia.

The cultural legacy of Sumer survived after the Kassites, but it survived not on the Babylonian plain, but in Assyria, whose story is told later on in this account.

A PICTORIAL
SURVEY
OF MESOPOTAMIA'S
HISTORY, ART,
AND ARCHITECTURE

*The photographic essay that follows depicts the objects and the scenes familiar to archaeologists as they dig amid the ancient ruins of Mesopotamia. The pictures illustrate the chief styles of art, craft, and architecture with which the people of Mesopotamia were involved during the more than three thousand years of their history. The artistic expressions of a people are motivated by many things, some of which are described in the pages following the photographs. In many cases the objects which represent these arts and crafts are virtually all that we have to evidence the accomplishments of cultures long dead. But a surviving art or craft may tell the archaeologist of a vanished people's aesthetics, of its vanities, its wealth, its skills, its religion, and its commerce. Thus it is sometimes possible to "resurrect" the dead. The photographs represent this kind of resurrection. They have been placed in chronological and topical order so that the reader may gain a hint as to the changing, teeming world which was ancient Mesopotamia, a world which lay at the very foundation of our own civilization.*

THE RIVER TIGRIS IN FLOOD. *The river has created a fertile plain rich in the minerals necessary to grow crops in abundance—the abundance which is a prerequisite to civilization. The Tigris—seen here in flood near the Assyrian site of Nimrud—and the plain together built the foundation of the Sumerian civilization—the world's earliest.*

Courtesy Dr. Vaughn E. Crawford

Courtesy The University Museum, University of Pennsylvania

PAINTED POTTERY OF THE PRE-SUMERIANS. *Deep in the earth under the ruins of the ancient cities of Sumeria, archaeologists have found the remains of the villages of the prehistoric farmers who first settled on the plain of Shinar. These farmers were skilled at pottery-making, and their fine painted vessels are often prized museum pieces.*

TEMPLE SUPERIMPOSED ON TEMPLE AT ANCIENT ERIDU. *The prehistoric farmers of Shinar built shrines to deities of fertility in the midst of their villages. As the villages grew larger, the shrines grew larger, until, after a thousand or so years, where there had been villages were cities and what had been shrines became temples served by myriads of priests and servants. The first shrine of the village is seen here at the bottom; the mighty ziggurat is at the top.*

Courtesy The Directorate General of Antiquities, Baghdad

Courtesy The Oriental Institute, University of Chicago

SUMERIAN STATUES EXCAVATED FROM THE SITE OF TELL ASMAR.

*Surprisingly little is known about the origins of the Sumerian people, although it is they who brought civilization into the world and laid the foundations for our modern way of life. The Sumerians carved statues of their gods, priests, and kings in their own likenesses: some bearded, some not; some in draped robes; some in wrap-around skirts. Their variety serves to suggest the teeming, busy world they lived in some forty-five hundred years ago.*

ourtesy The Oriental Institute, University of Chicago

THE GOD ABU.

PORTRAIT STATUE OF DUDEE, MINISTER AND
VISER AT THE ROYAL COURT OF LAGASH. *Some
the surviving statues of the Sumerians are p
traits. In the broad but not insensitive style of
Sumerian sculptor, the features of court lad
prime ministers, priests, kings, and nobles w
cut in soft stone. The spade of the archaeolog
in revealing these portraits of the men and wom
of the first civilization, is the magic wand t
re-creates an age.*

Courtesy The Directorate General of Antiquities, Baghdad

LIMESTONE HEAD FROM THE WORKSHOP OF A SCULPTOR OF URUK. *Sumerian sculptors were often master artists who were able to create wonderful works of art. There appears to have been a rather conventional and traditional art, such as that in the foregoing pictures, as well as a more naturalistic style, such as this limestone head. It is in this second style that the Sumerian sculptors often revealed their greatest talents.*

Courtesy The Directorate General of Antiquities, Baghdad

Courtesy The University Museum, University of Pennsylvania

THE GREAT ZIGGURAT AT UR. *The symbol of the Sumerian city was the ziggurat—at the center of the temple community, which was the heart of Sumerian society. Remnants of ziggurats still stand above the plain of Shinar, marking the sites of ancient cities.*

Courtesy The University Museum, University of Pennsylvania

HEADDRESS OF A LADY IN WAITING FOUND IN ONE OF THE SACRIFICIAL PITS OF UR. *The headdress, made of gold and semiprecious stones, is a delicate reminder of how far the Sumerians had progressed in achieving excellence in craftsmanship. The richness of the material and the skill of the artist combined to produce an ensemble modern ladies may well envy.*

Courtesy The University Museum, University of Pennsylvania

E STANDARD OF UR. *Life in ancient Sumer was an industrious d, more often than not, a prosperous affair. When the har- sts were good, there was leisure time for various pleasures. is scene, probably representing tribute brought to Ur as the sult of a victory over another city, shows some of the amen- es. In the upper register, a few distinguished citizens of Ur at their leisure quaffing wine, listening to music, and watch- g the scene before them. In the middle register, goats, sheep, ttle, and fish are brought before the conquerors. Below, bur- n-bearing slaves move between rows of onagers. In a land ere goods were valued as money, such scenes marked success.*

THE SKULL OF A LADY IN WAITING, COVERED BY ITS HEADDRESS, FOUND IN THE TOMB OF QUEEN SHUBAD AT UR. *When royalty died, or at the end of the new-year festival, certain individuals were chosen to accompany the deceased into an afterlife. The chosen, dressed in all their finery, were killed in the tomb and so interred. Millennia later, the archaeologist uncovers their remains. From the crushed and begrimed ruins, the archaeologist carefully, painstakingly restores the ancient finery to its former state, as in the previous illustration.*

Courtesy The University Museum, University of Pennsylvania

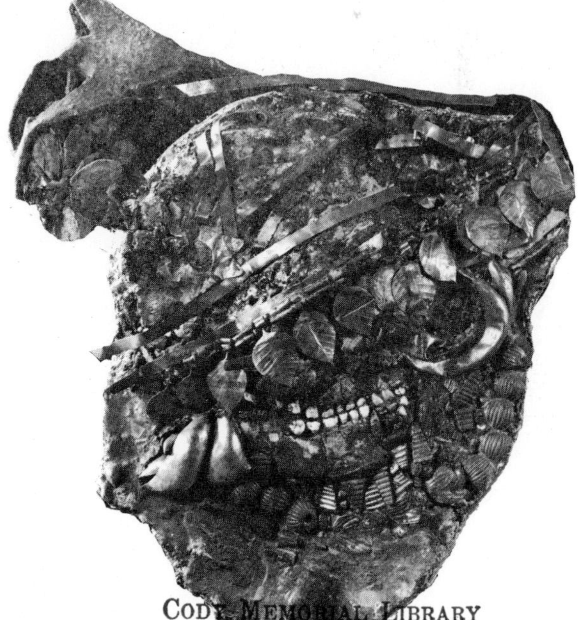

79985

CODY MEMORIAL LIBRARY
SOUTHWESTERN UNIVERSITY
GEORGETOWN, TEXAS

Courtesy The University Museum, University of Pennsylvania

THE "RAM IN THE THICKET" FOUND IN ONE OF THE DEATH PITS OF UR.

Courtesy The Directorate General of Antiquities, Baghdad

MINIATURE COPPER CHARIOT DRAWN BY ONAGERS.

*Delightful are those creations of ancient Sumeria which tell us just how well the Sumerian craftsmen observed the world around them and how, with humor and skill, they made use of their observations in wonderful works of metal and wood.*

A LYRE (RESTORED) FOUND IN ONE OF THE DEATH PITS OF UR. *The Sumerians, like people everywhere, enjoyed music, and it was only fitting that the musician and his lyre accompany the noble deceased into the other world.*

Courtesy The University Museum, University of Pennsylvania

**ⅠINDER SEAL IMPRESSIONS.** *The Sumerians were among the first to set forth the ɩ that a man's property was sacred unto himself even in his absence. The seal ɪression was used as a signature. It denoted the fact that when a man applied name to a thing it was as good as if he were eternally tied to the object, for signature was the mark of his presence. On the seal, the engraver drew heraldic ɩbols, sacred emblems, mythological scenes, and cuneiform writings, each in its ɩ way representing the individual owner.*

ˑtesy The Metropolitan Museum of Art, the Cesnola Collection, purchased by subscription, 1874–1876

Courtesy The University Museum, University of Pennsylvania

SCENE FROM THE WAR STANDARD FOUND AT UR.

*Along with the arts of peace, civilization brought better methods of waging war. At the very dawn of history, the Sumerians fought invaders and one another. Organized armies, headed by war chiefs, supported by soldiers in four-wheeled chariots, killed, ravaged, and destroyed what the arts of peace had built up. In the end, Sumeria, having trouble with its irrigation system and weakened by war, faded from history.*

SUMERIAN SPEARS AND DAGGERS.

Courtesy The Directorate General of Antiquities, Baghdad

Courtesy The Directorate General of Antiquities, Baghdad

BRONZE HEAD OF AN AKKADIAN RULER. *Sargon of Akkad conquered Sumeria and created an empire that may have stretched to the Mediterranean Sea. He was the first great conqueror of history, and though his empire collapsed soon after his death, his fame has survived the passing of centuries.*

Courtesy The Mansell Collection, London

KING HAMMURABI, STANDING BEFORE THE SUN GOD, RECEIVES HIS INSTRUCTIONS. *The fall of Sumer saw the rise of political power centered in the city of Babylon. One of the kings of Babylon was Hammurabi, whose inscribed stele was found by archaeologists in the nineteenth century. This stele set forth a code of laws that affected all walks of life. Though the laws were formulated before Hammurabi, apparently this was the first time in history that they were set forth as a unified graphic body.*

BOUNDARY STONE OF A KASSITE KING. *Little is known about the Kassites, the foreign invaders who conquered Mesopotamia and ruled for almost five hundred years. One thing is certain: the accomplishments of the Sumerians and the early Babylonians were not forgotten; for in the Assyrian period, which follows that of the Kassites, the older traditions flourished, although in new forms.*

Courtesy Trustees of the British Museum

GATES OF KHORSABAD FLANKED BY WINGED BULLS. *At the entrances to Assyrian palaces were placed great winged, human-headed bulls. These represented magical powers whose role was to guard the palaces from the entrance of evil spirits. Their massiveness and formidability are symbolic of the effect the Assyrians had on the rest of the Near East.*

Courtesy The Directorate General of Antiquities, Baghdad

STATUE OF ASSURNASIRPAL II FROM NIMRUD. *The representations of the Assyrians depict them as swarthy, heavy-set, and muscular; they were probably short in stature. Their descendants still survive among the modern Assyrians.*

Courtesy The Mansell Collection, London

KING SENNACHERIB'S CAVALRY IN THE MOUNTAINS.

Courtesy The Metropolitan Museum of Art, gift of John D. Rockefeller, Jr., 1933

A MEDE BRINGING TWO HORSES AS A TRIBUTE TO KING SARGON OF ASSYRIA.

Courtesy The Metropolitan Museum of Art, gift of John D. Rockefeller, Jr., 1933

*ancient Assyrians were clever ners and adroit merchants, but t of all they were celebrated and ed as soldiers. On wall after ntless wall of palaces and tem- in the Assyrian cities Nineveh, ırud, and Ashur, artists recorded stone the great wars of con- st which brought Assyrian ar- s from Egypt to Persia and enormous booty back to As- a. So real are the scenes of war some have called the Assyrian sts the first war correspondents.*

SACK OF THE CITY OF HAMAAN.

Courtesy The Mansell Collection, London

KING ASSURNASIRPAL II ENTHRONED IN STATE. *The king was an absolute monarch, traditionally regarded as gifted by the gods in the arts of war and peace and eternally under their protection.*

Courtesy The Mansell Collection, London

: BLACK OBELISK STELE OF SHALMANESER III. *The kings of Assyria commem-ted major events in their reigns in a number of ways—very frequently by ıns of small obelisks. King Shalmaneser III recorded on black stone his dis-ery of the sources of the Tigris River, a discovery which was made during a g military campaign in the mountains.*

Courtesy Musée du Louvre

ASSYRIAN PAINTED JAR.

Courtesy The Metropolitan Museum of Art, Dick Fund, 1951

*The riches gained by conquest greatly stimulate arts and crafts of Assyria. In ivory, wood, stone ceramic, craftsmen created lovely objects for pleasure of aristocrats and peasants alike.*

ASSYRIAN IVORY FROM NIMRUD.

Courtesy The Metropolitan Museum of Art, Rogers Fund, 195

*The Assyrians were athletic were keen lovers of sports. took pride in their success in ing, at which they were gr skilled. They, as with modern carried the process of destrc animals to its ultimate climax most complete extinction in where they once had been nu ous. The Assyrian artists ma cently recorded the fear and bravery of the animals and dramatic strokes portrayed death agony in a way that is ing even today.*

ASSURNASIRPAL II KILLING LIONS.

tesy The Mansell Collection, London

rtesy The Mansell Collection, London

WILD ASSES HUNTED WITH MASTIFFS.

Courtesy The Metropolitan Museum of Art, Rogers Fund, 1954

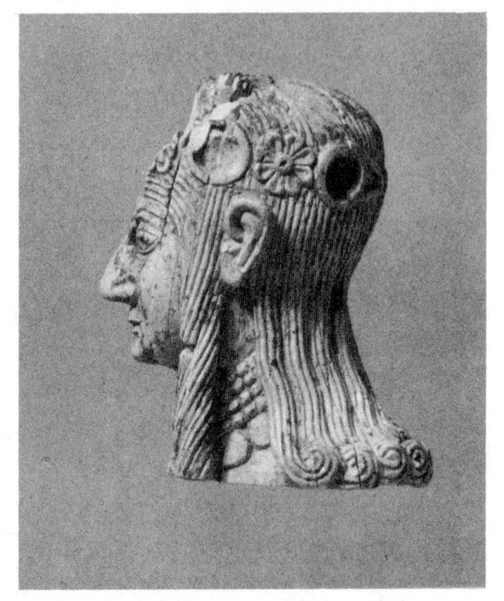

IVORY HEAD FROM THE BURNT PALACE OF NIMRUD. *Assyria, which rose to power by force, died in the fire of war. For centuries the great cities lay buried, and it has been only in the last hundred years that they have become known again—so terrible was the vengeance of the Persians, Scythians, and Babylonians. This small ivory head was found with other fine pieces in a well of a buried Assyrian palace.*

PANEL OF ENAMELED BRICK FROM THE PROCESSION STREET IN BABYLON BUILT BY KING NEBUCHADNEZZAR.



Courtesy The Metropolitan Museum of Art, Fletcher Fund,

From *Das Ischtar-Tor in Babylon* by Robert Koldewey, Leipzig, 1908

THE ISHTAR GATE OF BABYLON.

*a short time the Sumerian, Akkadian, and Assyrian ıral heritage was upheld in Mesopotamia after the fall he Assyrians. The Chaldean Babylonians, led by their t king, Nebuchadnezzar, built Babylon into a great ·opolis, the center of a mighty kingdom. Enormous s, ziggurats, palaces, monumental statues, and imperial ·essionways made Babylon one of the wonders of the ld.*

THE RUINS OF BABYLON—THE ISHTAR GATE. *But the splendors of Nebuchadnezzar's Babylon disappeared soon after his death—and with them, Mesopotamia's independence.*

Courtesy The Directorate General of Antiquities, Baghdad

ONE

# LIFE IN SUMER

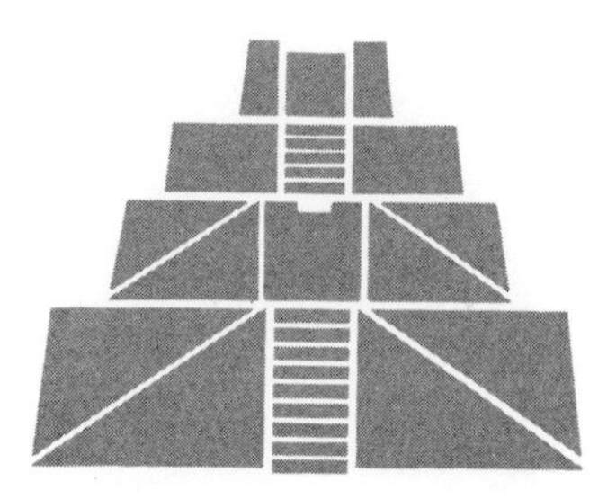

# 1. THE SUMERIAN CITY AND THE SUMERIAN HOME

The approach to a Sumerian city was a path across the green irrigated fields where farmers busily tended their crops. The path lay alongside an irrigation canal filled with the muddy waters of the Euphrates. Beaten hard by the sandaled feet of the passer-by and the tough little hoofs of heavily laden donkeys, the path wound between the irrigated fields. The low, flat-roofed houses built of brown sun-dried bricks appeared scattered at first, but they became more and more frequent, until the path was a street winding toward the center of the city.

It was this clustering of houses, and usually not any great city walls, that indicated the change from country to city.

The city houses had low doors and tiny barred windows. Mats and colored cloth, flowers and bright stones relieved the earthen brown of the brick walls. Bits of color could be seen here and there through open doors or on benches set in the sun. A corner of a sleeping rug might be seen hanging from the roof where a house's occupants had slept in the coolness of the night.

In a Sumerian city the streets were almost as noisy as they are in Iraq today. Herds of sheep and goats were driven along toward the temple, accompanied by yips from the shepherds; dogs barked, women gossiped, priests chanted, men talked, children played—and over all hung a pall of dust.

At the center of the city, to which all streets led, was the temple area. Here was the seat of the gods, the palace of the priest-king, the place of assembly, the temple factories, the storage bins, the warehouses—and, towering above all, the great squared-off platform on which rose one of the important temples. This platform was called a ziggurat, and it, more than anything else, can be said to symbolize ancient Sumeria.

Entering one of the houses in a Sumerian city, one had to stoop to avoid hitting against the low doorframe. The room one entered was generally not very large. Coming in from the glare of the sunny street, one needed a moment or two to get used to the interior, cool and barely lighted by several small screened windows high on the walls.

Soon, however, one could observe the clean reed matting on the floor, the mud brick with its covering of red-and-blue woven blankets along one wall, and the entrances to other, smaller rooms, which contained kitchen facilities, storage space, and so forth. Usually there was a small flight of stairs leading to the roof, where the householder and his family slept during the summer nights.

In a home belonging to a more well-to-do citizen, one might enter a central courtyard through an entrance hall. Around the courtyard would be the entrances to the service rooms, above would be a wooden balcony circling the court, and off this would be the bedrooms. Such buildings were common in the city of Ur during its Third Dynasty, around 1900 B.C.

Household shrines, where prayers were offered daily to invoke the care of the gods in human affairs, were not uncommon. In such shrines, the center of attraction was probably a seated statuette of the goddess Ningal, cut from limestone. Depicted with flounced skirt and flowing hair, she was a vision of piety. Frequently, the dead were buried beneath the floor of the shrine.

A visitor to the home of a well-to-do Sumerian would be served pomegranates, bread, and grapes. The lady of the house would wear her hair long, in the fashion of the image of the goddess. Her dress would be flounced, reaching to the ground. The upper part of her dress crossed over both shoulders, leaving a deep V at the neckline. Around the lady's neck would be a necklace of bright stones or perhaps white shells. The well-to-do men wore no beards; they used copper razors to keep their faces smooth. Unlike the priests, who wore their robes loosely thrown over one shoulder, the wealthy men wore a shirtlike garment wound around their waists, leaving their chests bare.

Women used malachite as a cosmetic to darken their eyelids; they had bronze mirrors which they used when applying it. A woman's day might include working with a slave to bring water from the well and grain from the temple granary, where the family allotment was issued, as well as caring for the children and supervising the preparation of food.

At supper, baked fish, unleavened bread, goat's milk, figs, dates, and grapes provided an ample repast, which the Sumerians consumed with their fingers. Everyone sat on mats, and the food was set on the floor in a variety of containers: baskets, pottery vessels, and excellent copper cups.

After dinner, sleeping mats were spread on the roof; and after a bit of gossip over the day's events, everyone slept under light blankets—the women apart, the men and slaves in their respective sections.

## 2. THE ZIGGURAT, CENTER OF THE SUMERIAN CITY

There is little question that the Bible story of the Tower of Babel, found in Genesis, refers to the ziggurats in the centers of Sumerian cities. The Bible says: "And the Lord came down to see the city and the tower, which the children of men builded."

The Sumerians, living on the endless flat plain of Shinar, had a very special regard for mountains, as it was from them that the waters of the rivers came, bringing life to the land. The Sumerians believed that a cosmic mountain, made up of heaven and air, sprang out of the primeval sea to begin the world.

Made up of the earth out of which crops grew, touching the heavens where the gods dwelt, the symbol of the mountains represented the center of mystery to the Sumerians. It was therefore fitting that on the flat plain on which they lived, the Sumerians built artificial mountains to show their respect. The ziggurat was the result.

The typical ziggurat, made up of hundreds of thousands of bricks, was square or rectangular at the base and had several stages, connected by staircases that rose majestically to the temple situated at the top. Even today these stairways can be seen at the ruins of Ur, where the best-preserved of the old ziggurats are found.

The mountainlike ziggurats were usually very large. The one at Ur, for example, measured 205 feet by 140 feet at the base and was three stories, or about 70 feet, high. The inside of the ziggurat of Ur consisted of layers upon layers of sun-dried bricks, and the entire exterior was covered with burnt brick laid in a bitumen mortar. It may well

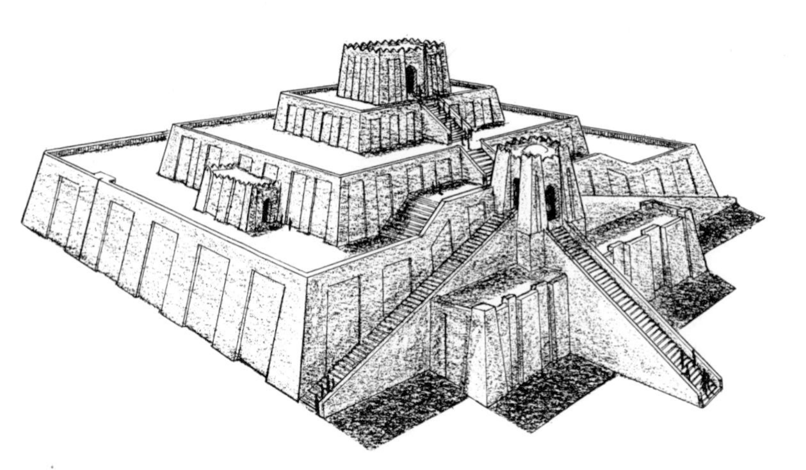

THE GREAT ZIGGURAT AT UR.

be that trees were planted on the terraces to give an even greater resemblance to the far-off mountains which the Sumerians believed were the original home of the gods.

Wherever the ziggurats existed (not all cities had them), an extraordinary amount of labor, skill, and patience had gone into their construction.

## 3. WITHIN THE TEMPLE COMPOUND

Surrounding the ziggurat and temple were low walls which enclosed not only the strictly religious buildings of the religious center, but also the shops and other buildings for different types of activities. The temple area was also the economic and social heart of the city.

Clustered around and within the walls of the temple were the buildings which housed the workrooms of the community craftsmen. Here the tanner prepared skins for use as containers, for military dress, or for the harnesses on the horses and donkeys used in war and peace. Potters spun clay on wheels and fashioned pottery vessels to be used in myriad ways. Carpenters made agricultural tools, wagons, and even ships. Coppersmiths pounded the raw metal into useful implements.

A widespread industry was wool-weaving. The sheep were sheared outside the temple grounds and the raw wool brought to the "factory." Though some weaving and spinning were done at home, a large percentage of Sumerian textiles were manufactured in the temple compound. Although men did some spinning, both spinning and weaving were usually carried on by women slaves. The carded wool was spun by means of a wooden spindle weighted with a whorl of clay or stone.

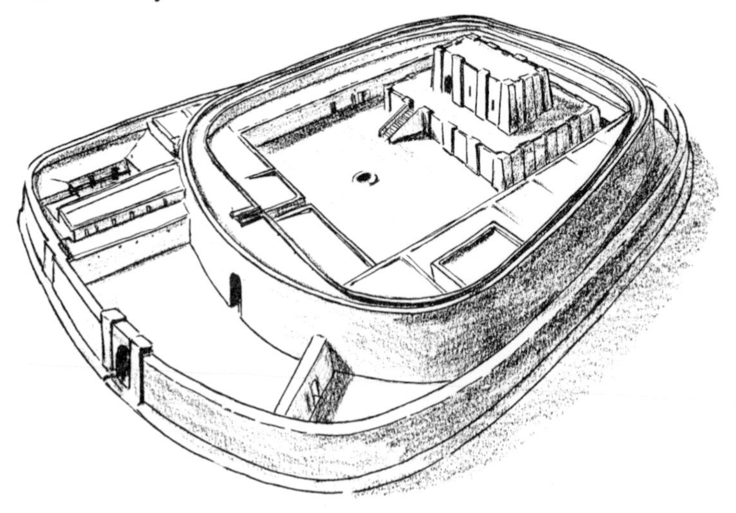

IN SOME CITIES, WALLS SURROUNDED THE ZIGGURAT AND THE ENTIRE TEMPLE AREA. SEEN IN THIS DRAWING IS A RECONSTRUCTION OF THE TEMPLE OVAL AT KHAFAJE.

Some of the temple wool, after being spun, may have been used for export to other lands and was probably one of the commodities exchanged for raw metal or luxury articles.

Weaving was done on a horizontal loom, and much of the completed cloth was very likely used for export too.

For every one of the items of merchandise, and there were a great many, accounts were kept in the temple area. Strict supervision by overseers and the detailed records kept by the temple scribes on tablets of clay ensured the security and efficiency of the craftsmen and the temple workers.

The record-keeping was a complicated business. For instance, barley grown in the fields was stored in the temple granary. Each month some of this barley was used in the temple kitchen and some was given to the temple brewers. The brewers not only made beer from the barley, but also were in charge of barley allotments for the goats, sheep, and cattle in the summer, when there was little grass. It was therefore necessary to write many records in order to keep a detailed account of what happened to the barley.

In addition to manufacturing and storing, the temple community controlled orchards, fishponds, river fishermen, and parish pigs. This control encompassed animal husbandry, including the crossing of the old stocks with new stocks to keep up the quality of the meat, milk, and hair.

The people of the temple were efficiently divided into teams or groups, each with its own foreman, and these groups were probably used as units of the army in wartime.

Everyone—officials, foremen, slaves, citizens, craftsmen, farmers, and so on—was under the administration of the priests of the temple. Each citizen had to do more than just his own farm work and manufacturing, since great emphasis was placed upon the community as a whole. In other words, he owed allegiance to the temple, the community, and to himself. It was this unity that kept the state strong and the individual responsible to his fellow man.

## 4. THE METAL SHOP

Among the crafts carried on in the temple area, metalworking was very important. The typical shop of the metalsmith was a very noisy place. In one corner a man might be pounding a sheet of copper into a bowl. The hammering caused the copper to bend and, at the same time, to harden. When it got too hard, the smith placed the sheet in the fire to soften it. Lifting it out again, he continued hammering until gradually a lovely deep copper bowl was produced. This process, known as annealing, is one of the oldest metalworking techniques.

In another part of the shop a group of workers might be preparing molds for casting a large statue of the goddess Ningal. If a wax image of the deity had just been completed, one of the workers would coat it with a very fine clay. Later the clay would have to be fired, causing it to harden and the wax to melt and flow from a hole prepared for it. The hollow clay mold was then ready for the pouring of the metal.

Outside the shop several men might be pumping air into a charcoal fire by means of a leather bellows. The heat had to be intense—so intense, in fact, that the copper in the crucible over the fire melted very rapidly. Once melted, it was poured into the hollow mold, creating an image in copper where once there had been one in wax.

Many were the demands Sumerian smiths had to fulfill: tools for the fields, weapons, objects for the temple, ornaments for people. Besides copper, some smiths worked in gold and silver, others in bronze.

The raw metal was allotted to the smiths by the temple community. It may originally have come from Arabia, Persia, or the highlands of Syria and Anatolia (which is the part of Turkey in western Asia equivalent to the peninsula of Asia Minor). In any case, the smiths were required to conserve as much of the metal as possible because of its high value. For this and other reasons, statues were cast with hollow insides by means of a clay core separated from the mold by spikes.

The smiths of Sumeria were fine craftsmen whose techniques, passed probably from father to son, helped lay the foundations of modern metallurgy.

## 5. FARMING

Just as the temple compound was the dominant aspect of Sumerian city life, the irrigation system was the most important part of the plain of Shinar and of Sumerian economy. The people of Sumer must have listed on tons of clay tablets the best methods of taking care of their irrigation system. Unfortunately, only a few of these tablets have survived.

The system consisted primarily of the main canal that

was fed by a weir, or dam, on the rivers. Off the main canal ran the feeder canals; and off these, even smaller feeders. Surrounding the fields were ditches; the little feeders that led into the fields could be controlled by removing or inserting clods of earth.

In fact, all the channels had gates by which they could be regulated. They all had to slope in given directions so that the water could flow. The waters were usually so muddy that they would silt up the channels, and these had to be continually cleared. The plain was so flat and the chances of flooding so great, especially in the spring, that dikes had to be built to hold the water back until it was needed.

All these projects needed constant attention, and a Sumerian farmer would advise his son to take care of the irrigation works first of all.

What a farmer did during the day depended on the season. In the summer he might be busy irrigating some of his fields. He would do this by opening the sluice off a main irrigation ditch so that water would flow into the appropriate feeder. Then he would take down a little bit of the mud wall of the feeder and allow the water to go into his field. When the field was flooded perhaps an inch or two deep, he would close the feeder wall with a shovelful of earth. The water would saturate the thirsty earth and nurture the growing grain.

In the spring a farmer and his son might be busy breaking up the earth with a pickax or a hoe in preparation for plowing.

The Sumerian plow was a very efficient piece of equipment. It was made of wood and had a metal point. A pair of stalwart oxen were yoked to it, and the farmer guided it by means of two handles behind. A boy might urge the oxen on with a whip or a stick or prevent the flies from clustering about man and beast with a branch.

The unique thing about the Sumerian farmer's plow was the seeder attached to it. This was simply a funnel with a tube leading down to the furrow. A man carrying a sack would walk alongside the plow and drop appropriate amounts of seed into the funnel. This ensured even distribution and expedited planting.

SUMERIAN FARMER GUIDING A PAIR OF OXEN YOKED TO A PLOW.

At harvesttime the farmers would work in teams: one man cutting the grain with a sickle, another binding the stalks.

Threshing involved riding over the stalks with sledges and then separating the grain from the earth and the stalks by tossing it in the air with pitchforks, just as is done in the fields today.

Grain was the basic staple of Babylonia, but beans, fruit, grapes, onions, radishes, and dates were also grown and enjoyed. The produce of Sumeria was abundant because the soil was so fertile that, when well watered and cultivated, it yielded a hundredfold return.

This gift of fertility was gratefully acknowledged as having come from the gods, and the Sumerian farmer never seemed to have forgotten this. Besides the formal temple ceremonies, there were daily prayers for luck during the day and festivals to celebrate the changing seasons.

## 6. THE SCHOOLS IN SUMER

Little would be known of Sumer today had the Sumerians not been exponents of the art of writing. They developed it from the simple drawing of pictures which conveyed ideas to a system of signs which represented spoken sounds but retained the use of some pictures. To write, they used a reed stylus with which they made wedge-shaped marks in soft clay. These wedge shapes are called cuneiform (from the Latin *cuneus,* meaning "wedge").

It took great skill to write cuneiform. The clay tablets, which were used while still soft, had to be handled carefully; the writing had to be precise and neat so that it could easily be read. There were so many combinations of signs to form the meanings that mastering writing was by no means easy.

In spite of these difficulties, the Sumerians were great recorders. Their lives were regulated by the written word: business accounts, religious rituals, grain storage, control of dikes and sluices, exchange of goods, taxes—all these and more were written down. The demand for men who were able to write must have always been very great. It is likely that this demand for scribes was the reason that the first schools were organized in Sumer.

In the beginning, these schools were probably part of

the temple community. A priest-scribe served as the instructor to students selected from the brightest and wealthiest of the city's youths. Strenuous vocabulary tests and long hours of copying the teacher's handwriting probably dominated the curriculum in the writing schools.

Later on in Sumerian history, schools were more elaborate. The growing knowledge of the world about them and the greater number of subjects that a scribe had to be familiar with very likely caused the schools to expand the curriculum. Knowledge gained by others was not only written down in the records of Sumeria, but passed on from

SCHOOLROOM WHERE SUMERIAN STUDENTS WERE TRAINED TO BECOME SCRIBES.

generation to generation through the schools as a legacy of the past. Mathematics, astronomy, horticulture, and religion were all part of the day's lessons.

Only the more well-to-do families could send boys to these schools. Tuition had to be paid in order to maintain the teachers, and, besides, the poorer families needed even the younger members for the day's labor.

Among the teachers there was a kind of headmaster, his assistant, several teachers for various subjects, classroom monitors, and a rather ominous but probably necessary "man in charge of the whip."

Creative writing seems to have been encouraged, for many examples of various versions of myths, legends, and history have come down to us. Charts and lists were compiled as teaching aids, and these must have been copied and recopied a thousand times over during the course of the school term, whatever its length.

The school consisted of rooms in which were rows of brick benches. Students probably straddled these as they pressed their wedge marks into the clay.

It took many years before a student could graduate and take his place as a respected, useful member of society. During those long years, working from dawn till dusk copying, recopying, memorizing, and being tested under the constant vigilance of a teacher who never "spared the rod," the Sumerians created an intelligent, disciplined class of able writers to whom they entrusted civilization as they knew it. This educational system is probably the prime reason that Sumerian culture had such a great influence on the ancient world, both when Sumeria flourished and for thousands of years after.

TWO

# SUMERIAN RELIGION AND SCIENCE

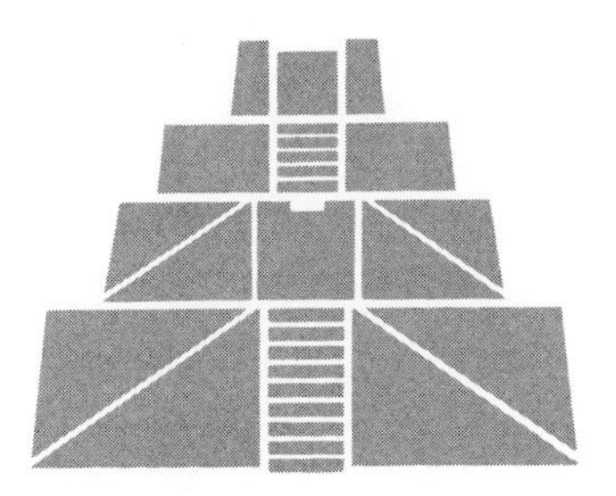

# 7. THE MYTHS

One of the great difficulties in trying to understand why the people of the far past acted as they did is the fact that all of us are living in a modern world in which a great many things are explained by science. If today one doesn't know such things as why it thunders during a storm or why plants grow as and when they do, it is not very difficult to find out—either by asking someone who knows or by going to a library and getting a book on the subject. For the Sumerians the answers to such questions came from the priests, whose job it was to understand the world around them, as far as this was possible. The priests knew such things as the proper time of year for planting, when to expect the rivers to flood, or what stars remained visible the year round; but their knowledge, fundamental as it was, was limited. Generally the priests and people adhered to one way of explaining the world, and that was by mythology—the stories of the adventures of the gods. Mythology was really science for ancient man, and it enabled him to describe natural phenomena in a manner perfectly satisfactory to him. The Sumerian account of the creation of the world and of man's place in it is a good example of how myths were used to make the world understandable.

The earth, according to Sumerian mythology, was like a flat plate floating in a primeval ocean. It was believed that below the earth was an underworld where the dead were entombed. Above was the sky, which, since it covered the world, was thought to rule it. The sky was the seat of ultimate authority, and in it dwelt Anu, the ruler of the gods.

Anu's right-hand man was Enlil, the god of the storm and the atmosphere. On the open plain of Sumeria, storms tended to be very violent. The winds caused great clouds of blinding dust to rise, heavy rain turned the land into a sea of sticky and treacherous mud, and the thunder and lightning were spectacular. Small wonder that Enlil was regarded by the Sumerians with awe and fear.

The earth was considered to be under the protection of the great mother goddess Nihmah, who gave birth to crops. She was the bringer of offspring, whether of man or beast, and was often depicted as a woman suckling her child. As such, she was also worshiped as the mother of the gods.

The favorite deity in this hot, dry land of the south was Enki, god of water. It was observed that when water touched the earth, plants sprang up as if the earth had been waiting to be fertilized. Moving water was thus thought of as a male force which, with the female earth, brought life to the world.

A great many gods were worshiped in Sumer—so many, in fact, that it would take a whole book, if not a library, to describe them and their powers. In addition, it was thought that in every object there were spirits which caused good or ill fortune at will. The copper a Sumerian used for tools, the wood for his house, the very pot he stored his grain in—all were supposed to be inhabited by forces which had to be recognized and dealt with. Such beliefs had the effect of making man seem very insignificant indeed. That is why the lives of the Sumerians centered around the temples and why so much of their labor was devoted to the gods.

## 8. THE GODS

It was only logical that when the early Sumerians watched the sun rise and set or noted the movement of the stars, the procession of seasons, and the life cycles of man and beast, they could sense order in the universe. Man himself, they believed, with all his tools and inventions, was a part of an ordered world. What was the reason for that order? The gods, they said, the gods who stood in the midst of the world, just as a farmer stood in the midst of his fields. The gods brought order out of chaos. If they failed in their duties, there would be catastrophe, just as there would be if a farmer failed to supervise his irrigation system.

The gods were depicted as manlike in appearance but immortal and all-powerful, as befit their status as rulers of the world. Each one had his task: there were gods of the pickax and the ditch as well as those of the sun and air.

The Sumerians had an account as to just how the world was created and order brought out of chaos. It was thought that in the beginning there was nothing but a primeval sea. Out of the sea sprang the cosmic mountain, which consisted of heaven, called An, and earth, called Ki. An and Ki were united as the mountain; between them they created Enlil, the god of the storm and the atmosphere, who then, it was believed, pulled the two apart, and thus the world was formed.

Enlil mated with the beautiful air goddess Ninlil, who bore him a son—the moon god Nanna. Nanna sailed across the sky in a gufa, the round boat made of wickerwork used by the Sumerians. Nanna became the father of the sun god Utu and of the stars and planets.

Enki, the water god, the lord of wisdom, was the true

organizer of the earth. Enlil appointed Enten the deity of farming and sent seed and agricultural tools to earth to help him.

This creativity was all very well, but the gods, it was believed, nonetheless had to labor every day to grow food for their sustenance. Even the immortals had to eat! The gods therefore pleaded with Nihmah, the creator goddess (who may also have been Ki, goddess of earth), to create man. With the help of Enki she fashioned man out of clay. Some say Enki caused men to sprout out of the earth like plants by opening the earth with a pickax.

Man was able to take advantage of the gifts of the gods because he was created for them. From them he learned justice, good deeds, kind acts, industry, love, and good conduct. If man had trouble it was because of his own misdoing, not the fault of the gods.

But because man was a child of the gods, he could pray to them and, if his words and acts were good, could expect them to help him. Here was the basic relationship between gods and man which Abraham must have known in his wanderings on the borders of Sumeria.

On a very ancient tablet, parts of a man's prayer to the gods are recorded:

> My god, the day shines bright over the land, for me the day is black. . . .
> My god, you who are my father who begot me, lift up my face. . . .
> The man—his god harkened to his better tears and weeping. . . .
> He turned the man's suffering into joy. . . .*

* S. N. Kramer, *From the Tablets of Sumer* (Indian Head, Colorado: Falcon's Wing Press, 1956), pp. 150–151.

# 9. THE DEATH PITS OF UR

Since man's actions and destiny were believed to be dependent on the favor of the gods, the Sumerians took part in many religious ceremonies and performed many rituals.

At the beginning of the new year, a festival was held throughout Sumer which was attended by the whole population of each city. The new year was the time when the fertility of the earth was ritually renewed. This was a most sacred festival, and it meant a great deal to the agricultural Sumerians.

According to one theory, the main participants were a young priest and a young priestess who were especially chosen. Apparently they were dressed and trained to represent the earth mother Ki and the deity of the water Enki. Amid great splendor they were led to the ziggurat in an elaborate procession. Then the two alone climbed to the top, where in the temple their union was consummated in the presence of a solitary priest. Held at the highest part of the city, next to the all-encompassing sky, the ritual symbolized the great need of man for the gift of the gods—fertility.

However, there was a sequel. The priest and his priestess had attained the highest posts in the state: they had acted as deities. Once the festival was over, their sacred functions were accomplished. But apparently their lives were also consummated at the top of the ziggurat, for it was supposed that life from then on could have no meaning for them. In any case, they were gently put to death, and with them the whole court of retainers—ladies in waiting, servants, soldiers, and even beasts—that had served them in the ritual.

The riches of craftsmanship and labor which represented the city were also part of this sacrifice to the gods.

A famous British archaeologist, Sir Leonard Woolley, digging at Ur in 1927, came upon what probably were the graves of such sacrificial victims. What he found was an astounding example of the elaborateness of these ancient rituals and how much they must have meant to the god-fearing Sumerians.

First Sir Leonard Woolley and the other excavators encountered a ramp leading down into a brick-lined pit. Toward the bottom of the ramp the skeletons of six soldiers were found. They wore copper helmets and held spears, apparently guarding the tomb. On the floor of the tomb, facing the ramp, two grooms stood at the head of a group of oxen. These were yoked to a pair of four-wheeled carts or chariots within which were the drivers. The reins were inlaid with silver and lapis lazuli and passed through silver rings.

The main tomb was at right angles to the ramp. Here were found the skeletons of more soldiers, complete with weapons, servants, and several harpists—their harps beautifully decorated with copper, silver, gold, and lapis inlay. Some of these harp decorations were in the form of bulls' heads.

At one end of the pit was a domed chamber with walls of limestone and a roof of burnt brick. Before this were a group of nine ladies, beautifully dressed in crimson robes, with headdresses of lapis and carnelian and leaf pendants of gold. Silver hairpieces with floral decorations, gold earrings, and gold and lapis necklaces completed what must have been a dazzling coiffure.

Inside the tomb was the remnant of the "king's" skeleton—that of the mock king who also took part in the ceremony—and, nearby, a lovely boat of silver, 2 feet long, stood against the wall.

In the priestess's chamber was found a wealth of rich jewelry: collars, pins, and amulets. She had apparently worn an elaborate wig decorated with rich gold ornaments of great delicacy. Next to her hand was a fine gold cup, and she had worn a cloak decorated with strings of gold, silver, agate, lapis, and carnelian beads.

Next to her bier were the skeletons of two women attendants. All about were such items as silver tables, lamps, silver vessels, a golden bowl, and—in true female fashion—some shells containing cosmetics.

Woolley found a number of these tombs, and the total impression of vast wealth and profound ritual is overwhelming.

In spite of the presence of all the dead victims, in some cases numbering more than fifty individuals, there is no indication of violence. It appears that each was prepared for the sacrifice, carefully dressed, and either drugged or poisoned in such a way that there was time to lie down and die yet not disturb a flower or piece of gold leaf from its place. Then the pit was filled in, and the gods and man renewed their union.

## 10. FORESEEING THE FUTURE AND THE BEGINNINGS OF ASTRONOMY

Since the Sumerians believed they were surrounded by gods whose will governed the present and the future, there were priests whose special job it was to read the signs in nature in order to foresee what the future held. Their methods varied, but one of the most important was liver divination.

Just as later peoples regarded the head as the place of thought and the heart as the seat of love, so the liver was considered by the Sumerians to be the seat of the emotions—the place where knowledge in its most sensitive form was supposed to have its home. If one sacrificed a sheep and examined its liver, it was thought that the signs revealed would enable one to predict the future. Every feature of the liver—lines, valleys, spots, wrinkles, and so on—had meaning; and a whole "science" of liver-reading was developed. By using liver divination, one could foresee the success or failure of any man-made project.

Another very important means of predicting events was by studying the stars. The Sumerians believed in astrology. Like all human beings, they were conscious of passing time, which they viewed as a progression from day to night or from season to season. Great floods and the reigns of ancient kings gave them a sense of history. The aging of individuals was another sign of passing time.

The priests divided the year into twelve units based upon the cycles of the moon, and the first appearance of the moon each month was celebrated with rituals. Eclipses were watched for with great zeal, since they were supposed to have great bearing on the affairs of men. Planets were representative of certain deities, and their qualities of good and evil had to be considered by king and peasant alike.

The clear nights characteristic of the Mesopotamian climate, coupled with the habit of sleeping on the roofs of houses, made the Sumerians very sky-conscious. The gods, whose homes were above the sky, were believed to have direct control over the stars and planets. An astrologer noting the movements of those heavenly bodies could therefore interpret the movements as indications of divine will and could act accordingly.

Out of observations for astrological purposes, the Sumerians probably developed a study of astronomy which included the mapping of stars and planets relative to one another. Such constellations as Orion, the Great Bear, and the Pleiades are readily recognizable on Sumerian astronomical charts and are in correct relation to one another. To further the accuracy of their charts, these astronomers located the signs of zodiac and marked the position of the stars along the ecliptic—the path followed by the sun on the celestial sphere.

Astronomy and astrology were thus closely linked—and the acts of men as closely governed—by celestial observations. One Babylonian stated:

"If the moon reaches the sun with faint illumination, one hour shading the other, justice will prevail in the land. The son will be faithful to the father." *

The Sumerians were in great awe of the surrounding universe and governed their acts accordingly. And partially because of this awe was born not only the science of astronomy and the development of the calendar, but also the methods of computing time and some aspects of mathematics, which obviously had to be used in their calculations. It is one of the wonders of human progress that often one people's superstitions lead to another people's science.

* Adapted from M. Jastrow, *The Civilizations of Babylonia and Assyria* (Philadelphia: J. B. Lippincott Co., 1915), p. 491.

THREE

# SOME KINGS OF SUMER, AKKAD, AND BABYLONIA

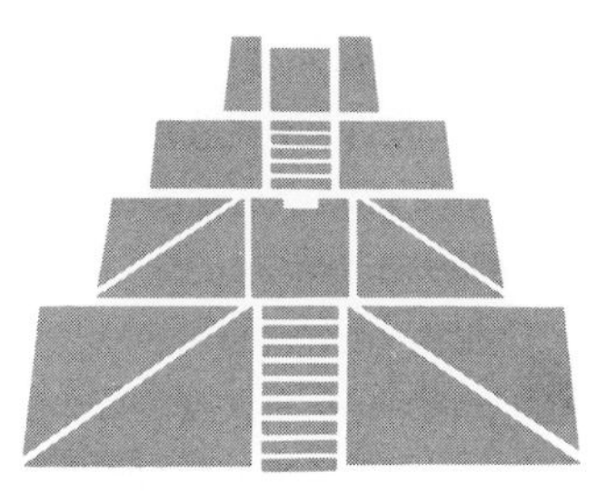

## 11. EARLY FORMS OF GOVERNMENT IN MESOPOTAMIA

In the prehistoric period before 3000 B.C., the people who lived in farming villages did not need very much government. Everyone had to do his part in carrying out the day's activities of farming, herding, cooking, building, and making things—otherwise the entire community would be affected. There was no time for idleness or the shirking of duty. Those who neglected some part of a duty out of forgetfulness or accident or for any other reason were ashamed of themselves when they realized what they had done. Their families and neighbors were ashamed of them as well. This sense of shame was so very strong that laws and written codes of behavior were not needed.

The earliest Sumerians were villagers, and moral behavior was all the law they needed to guide them. But this changed with the development of civilization. The way one acted in his daily affairs became less and less a matter of personal fear of doing something shameful and more and more a problem of society—a society that centered its activities in the temples. Everyone was a citizen not only of the city but of a temple community within the city, which might have several temple communities. A man might receive his land from a temple, to which he paid rent in the form of set amounts of his land's produce. The land owned by the temple was worked by everyone for the common good—in fact, this land was called common land. The seed and tools to be used in the common land were supplied by the temple, and tools could also be rented from the temple by farmers for tilling their own land.

The revenue gathered by the temple from the labors of the farmers and the skills of craftsmen was placed in storage magazines. Everything was duly recorded and itemized by officials appointed by the priests of the temple. In turn, the revenue was allotted according to the needs of the temple community.

Political control appears to have rested at first upon every citizen in an assembly. In early Sumer this assembly presumably would come together whenever there was need. The men would probably meet in a temple compound and as citizens argue the pros and cons of a question. There also seems to have been a council of elders who guided matters and probably were responsible for carrying out the will of the assembly.

In periods of trouble an individual was selected to act as leader. In time, the leader became the king. An important official, who often was made the leader during emergencies, was the chief official of the city's leading temple community. He was a most sacred individual and, as leader and city ruler, had a special name—*ensi*. Most of the troubles usually arose as a result of rivalry between cities; and during the wars that occurred, the ensi had absolute authority as ruler. At the end of the trouble, the ensi was supposed to step down and the assembly to take over control again. But wars raged on, emergencies persisted, and the ensi had to keep control; and in time the assembly grew less and less important. In the later periods of Sumerian history, the ensi set up dynasties, with the control passing from father to son. Thus the ensi was actually a king or lugal.

Around these kings sprang up courts with all necessary

(and sometimes unnecessary) officials and attendants, as well as relatives. Standing armies were at the ruler's service. And thus in later Sumer the system of government differed considerably from that of earlier periods.

But in spite of these changes, the number of revolts and the quantity of deposed rulers listed in the history of Sumeria indicate that the city thrones were never very secure places.

## 12. GILGAMESH

The kings of the cities of Sumer are known to us because they were listed on clay tablets by the later Sumerians. These tablets were afterward copied by the Babylonians and the Assyrians. Discoveries by archaeologists of some of the early tablets and the later copies place in our hands a list of kings whose reigns, according to the Sumerians, covered several hundred thousand years. For instance, the Sumerians listed eight kings whose reigns totaled 241,200 years! We know that, at best, these king lists cover not much more than a thousand years.

Some of the early kings were legendary, belonging more to mythology than to history. One such was Gilgamesh, king of the city of Erech, who was believed by the Sumerians to have been half god and half man and was the hero of a famous epic story.

Gilgamesh was a powerful king, greatly respected by his people. He had a close friend, Enkidu, who shared many adventures with him as they traveled here and there. One day Enkidu was killed, and the sorrowing Gilgamesh pondered the frailty of life. He wondered about his own mortality:

"Shall I not rise through all eternity?"

Desperately he set out on a journey to find Utnapishtim, a mortal who, it was believed, had been given eternal life. En route, Gilgamesh encountered many hazards, not the least being the warnings given by various gods that he was doomed to fail:

"Gilgamesh, where are you going? You seek life, but you will not find it. When the gods created man, they also gave man death; for only the gods hold immortal life."

Gilgamesh, however, eventually found Utnapishtim and asked him how he was given immortality. Utnapishtim told him that he originally came from the old city of Shuruppak on the banks of the Euphrates. For some reason, the gods were angry at the world and decided to destroy all life in it by sending a great flood.

One of the gods, Enki, took pity on the righteous Utnapishtim and secretly told him to build a ship:

"Bring into it the seed of all living things."

Utnapishtim built the ship, dividing it into seven decks, each with nine compartments. Into this ship he loaded his family and his animals. When the storm came all was in readiness:

"Six days and six nights raged the wind; the flood and the hurricane ravaged the land."

On the seventh day the storm ended, but the whole world was covered with water:

"I opened a window and the light fell on my cheek. I kneeled and sat down to weep, tears streaming on my cheeks. I looked on the quarters of the billowing sea."

The ship finally lodged on the peak of Mount Nisir

(probably the Biblical Ararat). Utnapishtim then sent out a dove to search for land, but it returned having found no place whereon to light. The same thing happened with a swallow. At last a raven found a place to land in the mud left by the receding waters.

In thankfulness Utnapishtim offered a sacrifice to the gods. But one of them, Enlil, was angry because someone had escaped. Enki again saved Utnapishtim by pointing out that it would have been wrong to kill the good with the evil. Enlil agreed and blessed Utnapishtim and his wife with immortality:

"Once Utnapishtim was a man, but now he and his wife shall be like the gods."

Utnapishtim tried to aid Gilgamesh by telling him how to find the plant of life. But Gilgamesh, though successful in getting it, lost it through theft and returned to Erech despairingly.

Even today one can feel closely akin to Gilgamesh and his troubles because they are perfectly human and understandable. His story is one of the world's oldest and another example of the Sumerian heritage and influence. There seems little doubt that Utnapishtim (sometimes called Ziusudra) was the model for the Biblical Noah. As for the flood, the low flat plain of Shinar had always been subject to flooding by the rise of the two rivers. Excavations at the city of Ur in the 1920's revealed, deep down at the prehistoric levels, an 8-foot-deep deposit of clay that marked one of these ancient floods. Floods which occurred later, at the beginning of Sumerian times, have left their traces in the old city of Kish and even in Utnapishtim's home town of Shuruppak. So there is some evidence for the story, even though we know that the Deluge was not world-wide. Yet to the Sumerian, his city and land were the world; for him the flood that engulfed them would truly bring an end to life.

## 13. SARGON OF AKKAD

Although the Sumerians made great progress in controlling nature, they were apparently much less successful with man. Even the earliest records of Sumer contain accounts of conflict among individuals and among cities.

For example, the shell figures on an inlaid wooden standard found in one of the tombs at Ur illustrate an ancient war. Four-wheeled chariots drawn by donkeys carry soldiers bearing spears and axes into action. Helmeted infantrymen with long spears herd prisoners along, while a few other soldiers dispatch fallen enemies with clubs. A scene of horror, it differs only in details of equipment from similar scenes in any war.

There was never any real unity in Sumer, even though one city-state might dominate the others for a while. Jealousies over land or water rights, and possibly over the control of overland or river trade, plus the age-old ambitions of man led to almost unceasing conflict.

Outside people, like the Elamites of Persia and the Guti of the Zagros Mountains on the north and east, often took advantage of this disunity to raid and destroy. A people who spoke a Semitic language, probably peasants and shepherds from Syria, settled around Babylon and made their center there. They called themselves Akkadians; and it was one of their number, Sargon, who, around 2050 B.C., became the first great conqueror of history.

Sargon started as a cupbearer to the Sumerian governor of Kish, but he soon led a revolt which made him king over Kish and a number of nearby cities. Quickly he attacked the warlike peoples in Assyria and Syria, winning their allegiance. Then he fell upon southern Sumeria and captured all the cities there, including Ur. Sargon, though Akkadian, adopted Sumerian customs and beliefs, at least for a while.

Not content with controlling Babylonia and Assyria, Sargon marched here and there conquering far afield. He overran Elam and even reached the eastern Mediterranean coast, where he is supposed to have colonized the region that is now Lebanon. In any case, Sargon became a legend; and many places that he is unlikely to have reached—even the island of Cyprus in the eastern Mediterranean—have claimed his presence.

But Sargon was not capable of controlling the Sumerians. They rebelled, and one of them murdered him. However, the fact that his successors reigned for some years after him was a tribute to the effectiveness of his conquests. From Sargon's time on, the land of the two rivers was known to the ancients as Babylonia, and this too demonstrates the impression the Akkadian ruler of Babylon had made upon the land and the people.

## 14. HAMMURABI

After Sargon's empire ended, in 1960 B.C., there was a brief revival of Sumerian political power centered in Ur, but it did not last long. A people called Amorites, who spoke a Semitic language, infiltrated the area around Babylon and gradually gained power. By 1800 B.C. they were in control of the whole of Babylonia and of some portions of Sargon's foreign empire. These Amorites were the founders of the First Dynasty of Babylon, which lasted from 1800 to 1550 B.C. One of their rulers, King Hammurabi, who ascended to the throne in 1728 B.C. was noted for his organization of the state and his excellent administration.

In December, 1901, a French archaeological expedition digging at Susa in Elam, the ancient kingdom in southwest Asia at the head of the Persian Gulf, found an 8-foot-high block of black stone. This block is covered with cuneiform writing arranged in vertical columns. At the top of the block there is a relief showing King Hammurabi in the act of receiving something from a sun god. What he was receiving was the code of laws written so elaborately on the body of the block.

This code is one of the more significant documents preserved from ancient times. In it are listed the rights and the penalties of the early Babylonians in the eyes of God and man. It deals with the treatment of one's fellow men, of women, of slaves, and of property. Damage was to be paid for by the damager; crime was punished by the state.

It appears that the bulk of these laws were not new but were derived from laws written down by the Sumerians in an earlier period. Hammurabi, however, brought them together into a code and had it written down, beginning his code with the statement:

"The righteous laws, which Hammurabi, the wise king, established and by which he stabilized the land and kept the government uncorrupt."

The laws were very strict and most efficient. For instance, if a builder were hired to build a house and the wall collapsed, he had to replace the wall without question. If the falling wall killed the owner, the builder was put to death.

The laws pertaining to a physician's practice were equally severe. If he operated on a man to save his life and succeeded he was paid handsomely. On the other hand, if the patient died, the physician's fingers were cut off!

Laws governing the family clearly reinforced family morality and the importance of the family in daily life. If a man died without a will, the state made sure that his widow and children inherited his estates. The rights of women, children, and slaves were recognized, and maltreatment of members of these groups brought penalties ranging from fines to death.

The principal concern seems to have been property rights, particularly land, crops, and irrigation—which is not surprising considering how much the people depended on these.

One rather remarkable section of the code has to do with giving false testimony. The laws against bearing false witness were so firm that the judge of the case was not allowed to change his decision without paying penalties for his original misjudgment.

The law courts were ready to hear both sides of a case, and the judges, presumably appointed by the king, had to rule in compliance with the code.

All in all, the code demonstrates the basic wisdom of the time and reveals much the same basic attitude that is found in modern democracies: a man is innocent until proved guilty. The fact that Hammurabi's code emphasizes this need for proof makes it a milestone on man's long road to true justice.

## 15. HAMMURABI'S BABYLON

Life in Mesopotamia changed considerably during Hammurabi's rule. And this was so not only because a dynasty of non-Sumerians reigned, but particularly because the whole structure of society was changing. No longer did the temple community dominate the life of individuals. Slaves captured in foreign wars became important in the economy, and as a result slave owners who had large estates were able to play a more important part in political life than had the single citizen with his lone plot of land. The citizens' assembly no longer had any power. The king was sole ruler and passed that rule on to his son.

Even the Sumerian language was falling into disuse, and the Semitic tongues of the Near East were being employed more and more in commerce and in rituals.

The Sumerians themselves seem to be disappearing as they mixed with the foreigners.

A most significant change was in the concept and knowledge which the people of Mesopotamia had regarding the world. Not even in Sargon of Akkad's day had there been such awareness of other lands and peoples. The traders who came to the markets of Babylon came from as far away as Egypt, where the splendid days of the Middle Kingdom (2150–1785 B.C.) were just ending. The strange world of India to the east was represented, perhaps in the form of cotton cloth or elaborate feather work. From the west, the island of Crete in the Aegean Sea furnished beautiful pottery and unusual beads, while fine wool from Anatolia and Persia was in increasing demand.

In the Persian Gulf the islands of Bahrein were the source of pearls, and it is even thought that lapis lazuli was imported from as far away as the borders of western China. It was a truly international world—and Babylon was at almost its exact center.

In such a world, gold and silver were increasingly recognized as useful for measuring the value of goods and therefore as mediums of exchange. The Sumerians had introduced many standards of measurement, and in the days of Hammurabi there existed measured containers for transferring products such as grain and oil. Devices for measuring the length of articles such as cloth and wood were also in use. A common practice—one that is still used in the East—was to place a number of weights with fixed values in one pan of a scale in order to measure goods placed in the other pan. Silver and gold were generally measured in this way.

The Babylon of Hammurabi must surely have been the kind of noisy, bustling city one still expects to encounter in Asia. Hammurabi is said to have straightened the streets and introduced town planning—perhaps after learning the success with which it had been carried out in India. Unfortunately, much of Hammurabi's Babylon was dismantled by later monarchs as they created an even more bustling and grandiose city.

With Hammurabi's Babylon we have come to the end of the early period of the Mesopotamian world. The next five hundred years or so are shrouded in mystery. We do know that the easily accessible open plain of Babylonia's two rivers, with its riches of civilization, was a continual temptation to the barbaric peoples of the surrounding deserts and mountains.

Many of these barbarians conquered Babylonia, only to be absorbed by the civilization they had defeated. They became, as it were, as Babylonian as the Babylonians, adopting their clothing, food, and even their gods. Then a new group of barbarians would in turn conquer the land, and the process would start all over again.

All these upheavals made it even more difficult to give the land the care it needed if it was to bear fruit. If an enemy invasion caused the canals to be neglected, disastrous famine and poverty soon followed. Added to this finally were the confusion and disruption resulting from the petty squabbles within the country itself.

The story of early Mesopotamia is one of splendid accomplishment in creating a remarkable civilization and maintaining it for so long. It is, in fact, a good example of man's solving the problems of the land and world he lives in but not those of his own nature.

FOUR

# THE ASSYRIANS

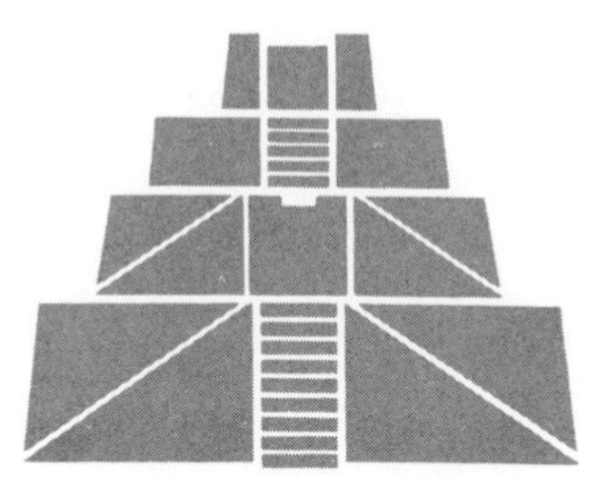

# 16. ASSYRIA, THE VULNERABLE LAND

Where the Tigris River comes out of the mountains and starts its long meandering course toward the flat plain of Babylonia, there is a country of rolling hills and fertile valleys. Here the winter rains provide water for rich crops of grain and grapes in the valley fields, while the hills in spring are covered with lush grass and the mountain slopes with forests of poplar, oak, and pine. This is the country of the Assyrians, a swarthy, stocky, Semitic-language-speaking people who for more than three hundred years dominated the Near East in a fashion never before known.

South of the point of the triangle made by the Tigris and its tributary, the Greater Zab River, there is a gravelly open desert which stretches in barren miles almost to Babylon. This waste clearly separates the rich Babylonian plain from Assyria. The other boundaries are the mountains that curve around the country like the shores of a bay.

The great cities of Assyria were Ashur and Nineveh. These places were trading centers long before they were capitals of an empire. Here the wild mountaineers could trade with the shepherds and farmers of the hills and valleys. Here too the manufactured produce of Babylonia could be brought by caravan and exchanged for raw materials such as stone, metal, and wool.

Assyria was a good place to live in. The rich grass fed enormous flocks of fat, woolly sheep; the fertile rain-watered valleys did not need much irrigation to produce grain and fruit; and the far-flung trade which passed across the land brought the fine manufactures of the known world. But there

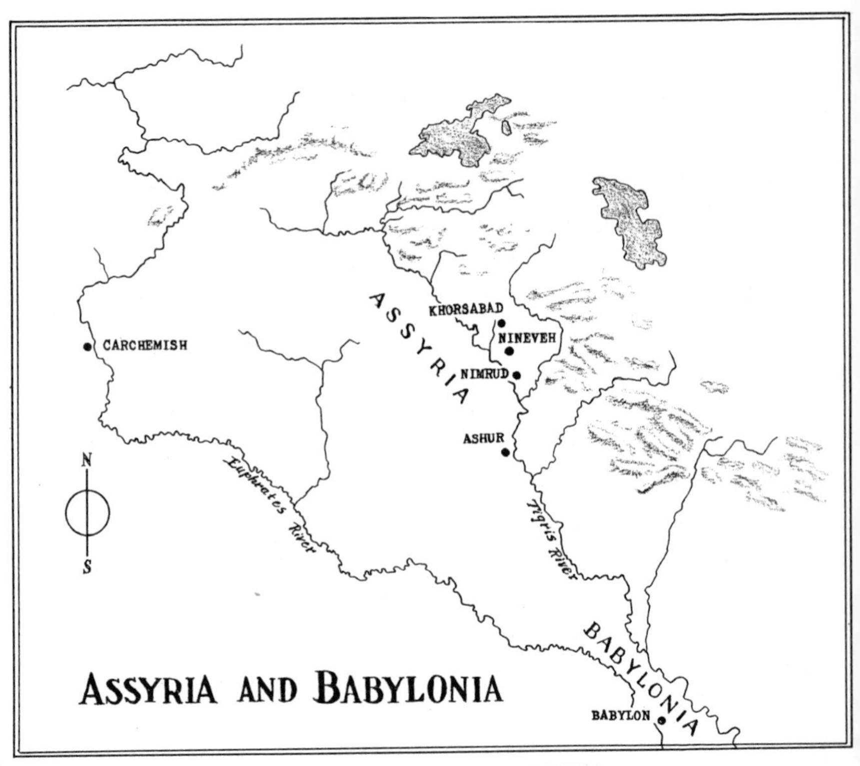


MAP OF ASSYRIA AND BABYLONIA.

was one fatal difficulty: Assyria was a vulnerable country. With few natural defenses and subject to the jealousies of its neighbors, the country knew little peace in its formative years. If it wasn't the mountaineer tribes who invaded for loot, it was the Bedouins—the nomadic Arab tribes of the desert—the Sumerians, or the Kassites—a people from Iran who ruled in Mesopotamia from 1550 to 1170 B.C. Fierce wars were continually being fought, and the Assyrian peasants learned to use the hoe and the sword, the spear and the shepherd's crook with equal dexterity.

The centuries of conflict could have only one effect. Forced to improve their military status for defensive reasons, the Assyrians developed the ancient East's most powerful and ruthless army. It was war that made them survive, and it was war that created their great empire.

## 17. THE TYRANNY OF THE ARMY

The war-toughened peasants of Assyria were among the ancient world's finest bowmen. They formed the infantry backbone of the army. Capable of launching flights of well-placed arrows to meet an attack or of accurately picking off the defenders on a city's walls, they were difficult for the enemies of Assyria to defeat. The archers were backed up by powerful spearmen and shield carriers who fought at close quarters. Then there were the heavy chariots and the horsemen who attacked with tremendous speed and power, maneuvering with great skill in compact units through and around enemy formations. Siege equipment was highly developed: wheeled rams were drawn up to the walls of a city and with great blows breaches were smashed through stone and brick.

All these military forces were used with skill and ferocity by the Assyrian rulers. It was not only the form of the army that gave it such terrible success in war, but also the fact that for the first time in the ancient world iron was used to make most of the weapons.

Against iron spears and swords, bronze shields were useless. Nothing then used could withstand the tough, sharp edges and points of the Assyrian weapons. When the Assyrians first attacked their enemies with these awesome novelties of war, it caused almost as profound a reaction as the atom bomb has in our own time.

Fear was a weapon well understood by the Assyrians and used by them as effectively as bows and spears. Their treatment of defeated enemies was as ruthless and terrible as any in history. When Assyria's King Assurnasirpal (883–859 B.C.) * defeated a group of rebellious princes in Syria, he wanted to make an example of them in order to prevent future revolts. He described their punishment and had the description publicly displayed on the walls of the city buildings:

"I erected a pillar opposite his city gate; all the chiefs who had revolted I flayed; with their skins I covered the pillar; some in the midst I walled up, others on the pillar I impaled on stakes, still others I arranged around the pillar on stakes. Many within the borders I flayed; with their skins I covered the walls."

Not content with severe measures like these, the Assyrians developed the plan of transporting whole cities or tribes to places remote from their homelands. By so doing, they removed potential rebels from their strongholds and settled in their place people who had only the Assyrians to depend on for security in their new homes. Thus, for example, we find the Hittites, the mountain tribes from the plateau of Anatolia, pining on the hot plains of Babylonia, while men of the plains shivered in the mountains of Armenia in western Asia. The Assyrian sculptors loved to depict in bas-relief on the walls of palaces the melancholy

* Dates following the names of kings refer to the period of their reign.

processions of people making their dreary way across deserts and mountains far from their homes.

The Assyrian forces, in a space of about four hundred years, created an empire that included parts of Persia and Anatolia and all of Babylonia, Syria, Palestine, and Egypt. The treasures of the ancient world were carried to Nineveh, Ashur, and the palace city of Khorsabad. Slave labor created massive buildings that were among the wonders of the East; these included temples and palaces filled with magnificent stone carvings depicting Assyrian victories.

But in spite of the savage way the Assyrians suppressed revolts, the nations of the ancient world rebelled again and again. No Assyrian king could rest easily on his throne. Almost the first thing a new king had to do was to lead an army against rebellion. This continual application of force eventually doomed the Assyrian empire, thus providing a lesson for rulers of other nations and empires to come.

## 18. THE SPLENDOR OF THE KINGS

But in the days of its power, Assyria was an imperial world of incredible splendor.

In the middle of the nineteenth century the civilized world was astounded by reports coming from the Near East. One account after another told of the finding of great palaces and temples in the huge mounds that stood close to the Tigris near the modern city of Mosul in northern Iraq. Some of the palaces were hundreds of yards in dimension and filled with vast numbers of rooms, passages, and courtyards. Corridors stretched for hundreds of feet in many directions, and every foot of their walls was lined with magnificent stone reliefs. These sculptures depicted daily life in ancient Assyria, palace receptions, military campaigns, religious rites, the tribute of subject natives, and the vast wealth of a great empire. Enormous stone bulls and lions guarded the palace entrances. When the heads of some of these appeared by grace of the excavators' shovels, the native workmen fled in astonishment and fear, as if a world of monsters had come out of the past.

As archaeologists probed deeper into these mounds, the treasures of the past were revealed in even greater number: magnificent carved ivories and rooms filled with clay tablets on which were written the records of empires and kingdoms. Carved on a black stone obelisk of Assyria's King Shalmaneser III (858–824 B.C.) was a list of the tribute of the kings of the empire. One of these kings was Jehu, son of Omri, king of Judah in southern Palestine, who is mentioned in the Old Testament. This information provided a substantial link with the Bible and increased the interest in Assyria, which is still maintained up to the present day as archaeologists continue to uncover the astounding wealth of the Assyrian kings.

## 19. LIFE IN ANCIENT ASSYRIA

The culture of the Assyrians was largely borrowed from neighboring areas, especially from Babylonia. The Assyrians recognized many of the Sumerian gods and built ziggurats to worship them. Nevertheless, Assyrian religion was not quite the same as Babylonian or Sumerian. The chief god was Ashur, who was lord of all things. Ashur had fought with and defeated Tiamat, the hideous monster of chaos, and brought the world into being. As lord of heaven and earth, Ashur was the most powerful of all gods, and, of course, the kings of Assyria were regarded as having close connections with him.

In fact, the king was regarded by the people as a god—a god on earth whose duties included bringing the good will of the heavenly gods to Assyria. Assyrian kings were bound by religious customs, and these customs were not easy to observe. Five days a month, wherever he was, the king had to fast and perform certain ceremonies. On the first day of the new year, he went without food and water until the rise of the new moon in the evening.

No matter how arduous a military campaign might be, the king's presence was required to bring good fortune in war. He was also the first judge in the land and could be appealed to as a last resort. It was up to the king to supervise canal-building and to ensure the well-being of the farmers and shepherds upon whom the economy depended. In fact, the king was frequently called "the good shepherd, the one who fears the great gods, who guards the truth, who loves the right, who renders help."

The mother goddess Ishtar was one of the most popular deities. She was both the goddess of love and fertility and the mistress of battle. The Assyrians always invoked her before their campaigns. Only Ashur—her husband and brother—was more powerful.

Many deities were worshiped in Assyria, and a number of their functions related to agriculture, herding, and war, the chief concerns of the people. The Assyrians were great believers in omens and used oracles and seers to interpret the signs of the gods. As with the Sumerians centuries earlier, liver divination was regarded as the best method of predicting the future.

There were terrible demons described in Assyrian mythology, and earth-shaking battles were fought between them and deities of good. In such battles, man's fate was seriously involved.

Death was a dreadful thing, for the underworld was a gloomy place where the shades of the dead wandered aimlessly with little to comfort them. As if to offset this fate a little, the dead were buried under the floor of their houses, usually in family vaults. The bodies were placed in sarcophagi (stone coffins), and nearby were left a few dishes and jugs to hold food for the afterlife. A lamp was always left burning in the tomb to mitigate the darkness.

The wonderful stone reliefs tell us a great deal about Assyrian ceremonies and military practices, but only sketchy details of Assyrian daily life are known. It is certain that the Assyrians had developed a method of irrigation and that

ASSYRIAN METHOD OF LIFTING WATER FROM THE RIVER TO AN IRRIGATION DITCH.

many of the people lived in small mud villages in the midst of the fields, just as do the peasants of that part of Asia today, but there is little left to tell us of that life.

HEAD OF AN ASSYRIAN.

A very large percentage of the population lived in the cities, where they carried on trade and maintained crafts. Many were certainly needed in government offices, and the king's retainers must have been numbered in the thousands. Townspeople lived in brick houses with flat roofs, much as in Babylonia. The streets between blocks of houses were laid out in a checkerboard pattern, and in Ashur these were placed diagonally to the points of the compass in order to obtain shade. All streets led to squares and to the gates of the city wall—favorite meeting places. The streets themselves were paved with cobbles or blocks of stone, and provision was made for drainage.

Assyrian town houses were built around an open court, in the corners of which could be found a well, an oven, and a grinding stone for making flour. Around the court were rooms for dining, sleeping, and leisure. A vestibule passage led to the street, and off this was a large reception room for guests. This tended to be well decorated with wall painting, hangings, and fine rugs. In each room were niches for lamps and personal belongings. A stairway in one of the main rooms led to the roof, where on hot summer nights the family slept under the stars.

In the homes of the more well-to-do, there were bathrooms with asphalt floors and drains to carry off the water. These bathrooms are symbolic of the excellent technology of the Assyrians, whose practical understanding of city life helped prepare the way for cities to come.

At home, food was usually plentiful. For the poorer population, bread, dates, fruit, honey, and goat's milk were staples; while mutton, chicken, pork, and kid were added to the diet of the more well-to-do. Wine was drunk on every festive occasion.

Clothing was usually of wool, though linens and cotton had some vogue among the upper classes. Purple apparently was a favorite color, and imports of dye were brought from Phoenicia.

The city bazaars were active, noisy places where all the languages of the known world were spoken by traders, slaves, and citizens alike. Virtually anything could be obtained in the markets of royal cities like Nineveh and Ashur, whether it was Egyptian linen, Red Sea pearls, or Anatolian iron weapons. Many craftsmen resided in the cities, and they lived in various quarters according to their specialties. In these quarters the streets were lined with the stalls of the shopkeepers, who sold the bronzes, pottery, woven garments, and other objects made there.

Much of the business that was transacted in these places was written down on clay tablets in the same method the Sumerians had used. But now the cuneiform writing was more simplified, and this reduction of signs and symbols greatly expedited the preparation of accounts and contracts.

The Assyrians had a good deal of respect for the practical wisdom of the past and especially for that of the Sumerians. Assyria's King Sargon II (721–705 B.C.) formed a small library of Sumerian and Babylonian tablets or made copies of the ones then in existence. Very likely, private individuals did the same thing. However, it was King Ashurbanipal (668–626 B.C.) who created a royal library of tremendous scope and importance. Having learned to read Sumerian when he was crown prince, he devoted many hours to the reading of the old records. He even had dictionaries of Assyrian and Sumerian prepared.

In 1849, Sir Henry Layard, a British pioneer archaeologist working for the British Museum, was digging in the mound that marked the royal palace of Ashurbanipal of Nineveh. One day his diggers encountered two large chambers of the palace in which were piled clay tablets a foot or more in depth. More than twenty thousand tablets were found, each one related to some aspect of life in the ancient world. The Assyrian king's interests were very broad. A catalogue of his library includes such subjects as medicine, botany, astronomy, astrology, chemistry, metallurgy, lexicography, mythology, business, literature, and history. Ever since the discovery, scholars have toiled over this fantastic treasure-trove of ancient knowledge that reveals the extent of two thousand years of human endeavor by the shores of the Tigris and Euphrates.

## 20. THE FALL OF NINEVEH

Among historians, the Assyrians have been the subject of much controversy. Some, looking only at their record of war and brutality, condemn them as having contributed nothing to civilization except the art of all-out war. Others, more familiar with the true situation of the Assyrians in the ancient world, give them great credit for having brought together a considerable part of the world's learning, which has been passed on to later peoples.

The world that the Assyrians knew was a violent one. Surrounded by hostile states on all sides, invaded continually, the Assyrians, whether they wanted to or not, had to fight to survive. Under kings made famous by being mentioned in the Bible—for example, Ashurbanipal, Sargon II (721–705 B.C.), and Sennacherib (705–681 B.C.)—they conquered most of their enemies. With the great mass of captive labor they had acquired by conquest, they created enormous cities filled with great temples and palaces. Assyrian garrisons guarded the conquered areas, and the Assyrian army was prepared to march wherever danger beckoned.

Taxation in Assyria was heavy. The support of the army

was a continuing burden. At first the army was made up of volunteer farmers who joined to protect their land. Later, with the conquest of an empire and continual wars, a standing army had to be maintained. Not even the loot taken from conquered nations could pay the cost. In spite of military success, bribery, punishments, and alliances, the Assyrians were unable to avoid constant war. On the plateau of Persia, a nomadic, horse-riding people, the Medes, raided the eastern borders; the wandering, pastoral Scyths of the steppe country of the north invaded through the Armenian passes; the Egyptians, the Judeans and Israelites of Palestine, and the Babylonians revolted at every opportunity. Gradually the Assyrians were forced to retreat. After the death of Assyria's last great king, Ashurbanipal, in 626 B.C., the Assyrian empire shrank rapidly. Finally, in 612 B.C., Nineveh itself was taken by a coalition of Chaldean Babylonians and Medes, who breached the great walls and burned the city, leaving only shapeless heaps of rubble in which the bones of the Assyrians were cremated.

This event was celebrated in the Bible by more than one prophet. Ezekiel gave what was probably the most dramatic statement:

"Asshur is there and all her company: his graves are about him: all of them slain, fallen by the sword: Whose graves are set in the sides of the pit, and her company is round about her grave: all of them slain, fallen by the sword, which caused terror in the land of the living."

The fact that the Assyrian kings recorded their battles in such detail, as well as the fact that much of what we know about them comes from accounts given by their enemies, has warped their real role in the story of civilization. Wars are as savage now as they were then; the fact that the Assyrians perfected warfare for their own survival is hardly a condemnation. Certain it is that as long as the army was successful, there was security at home—a security that rarely lasted for long in the thousand years of Assyria's existence.

FIVE

# THE CHALDEAN BABYLONIANS

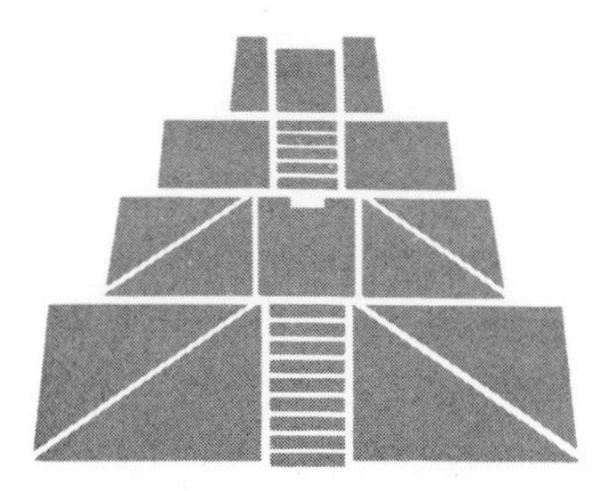

## 21. THE CHALDEAN WORLD

Amid the ashes of Nineveh, Nabopolasser (625–605 B.C.), the Chaldean king of Babylon, and Cyaxares (624–584 B.C.), king of Media, made a treaty. All the land in Assyria east and north of the Tigris was to belong to the Medes, the rest to the Chaldeans. The treaty was sealed by the marriage of the beautiful Amytis, granddaughter of Cyaxares, to Nebuchadnezzar, son of the Babylonian king. So began the more than seventy brilliant years (612–539 B.C.) that were to bring Babylon immortal fame as the most splendid city of the East.

The Chaldeans were a Semitic people who had settled in the fertile areas of southern Babylonia near the Persian Gulf around 1000 B.C. Because of their proximity to the sea, they were known as Sea-landers, and they were in constant rebellion against the Assyrian conquerors. Centuries of savage warfare and brutal retaliation had never daunted them. Toward the last, the Assyrians had to concede more and more to them, even appointing Chaldeans governors of Babylonian provinces in the Assyrian empire. It is no wonder that with the fall of Nineveh the Chaldeans exulted in their new power and created an empire of their own.

The energetic Prince Nebuchadnezzar swiftly seized Syria and Palestine, and was only stopped at the border of Egypt by the news that his father had died and that he was king. And what a king he made! During his reign (604–562 B.C.), a new Babylon was created by the shores of the Euphrates. Enormous walls were constructed to guard the city. As one passed through great gates, the roads into the city took one up magnificent processionways to dramatic groupings of palaces and temples. The most famous gate was that of Ishtar, which led to the Sacred Way. The gate was decorated with glazed brick of many colors. The walls were covered with reliefs of animals, real and mythical. Entrance was obtained through a great arched passageway flanked by castellated towers.

In one direction the way led to the great brick temples, the most famous of which was Etemenanki, dedicated to Marduk, patron god of Babylon. Seven stages high, it must have towered several hundred feet in the air—a landmark that could be seen for miles around.

In the other direction was the great palace of the king. In the midst of its grounds rose one of the Seven Wonders of the World—the Hanging Gardens.

As the story goes, Nebuchadnezzar loved his Median wife. Troubled by her longing for the forested mountains which were her home, he had constructed a man-made mountain to ease her homesickness. Not content with the brick which was the usual Babylonian building material, he had brought great hewn stones from the mountains and, in effect, raised a mountain on the plain. This building rose as a series of vaulted terraces, one above the other, to a height of perhaps 350 feet.

Around the building was a moat of flowing waters, while inside it deep wells fed water to hydraulic pumps that raised the water to a reservoir at the very top of the structure. On each terrace, deep layers of rich soil, moistened by the abundant water and warmed by the hot sun, supported a profusion of flowering trees and shrubs. Flowers scented the air, and graceful vines hung over the terrace walls. Beautifully decorated vaulted halls were filled with the treasures of an empire: the finest fabrics of Phoenicia, the silver vessels of Asia Minor, the wines of Palestine, the gold ornaments of Egypt. Slaves waited on guests who reclined on divans sipping the juice of pomegranates and other fruits, while below throbbed the teeming life of the great city. Such were the Hanging Gardens as travelers saw them, but as for the modern visitor who goes to the stupendous ruins of Babylon, no one—archaeologist or tourist guide—can point out to him the place where the gardens stood.

## 22. THE END OF BABYLON

Nebuchadnezzar did not give himself entirely over to luxury. He was a serious, intense man who tried to revive Babylonia as it had been before the ravages of the Kassites and Assyrians destroyed it. Because of his enterprise the canals were again filled with water and the fields of the flat plain of Shinar turned green once more. The temples in some of the ancient cities of Sumeria were restored and learning and the arts revived.

Chaldean culture was truly the culture of old Babylonia and Sumeria, but added to it were the changes of more recent times. Astronomy, for instance, was gradually moving away from being solely the tool of astrologers. The Chaldeans were increasingly aware of the value of astronomical observations to the accuracy of the calendar and to the reliable determination of direction on land and sea. Many of their studies were continued by the Greeks in later times and became the basis of modern astronomical science.

Artists, craftsmen, priests, and scholars—all contributed to the glory of Nebuchadnezzar's Babylon; and in the forty years of his reign, it appeared that the old civilization of the Tigris-Euphrates would again dominate the known world. Actually the new Babylon was the last phase of that civilization. For all its splendor, Babylon did not have the military strength to survive against the powerful enemies that gathered along its borders.

Twice during the reign of Nebuchadnezzar the kingdom of Judea had revolted, and twice the revolt had been put down. The second time, forty thousand Hebrews were exiled in Babylon, where they served as slaves and artisans. This was the great Babylonian exile that has never been forgotten by people of the Jewish faith, even to this day. A people totally and helplessly exiled from its homeland and serving foreign masters—this is a story that unfortunately is repeated again and again in history. Yet during that exile the Hebrews exhibited such faith in their God and such confidence in His help that it stands out as a remarkable example in history of a people's winning out over despair and tragedy. The unknown psalmist who lamented this exile is acknowledged to have written one of the most poignant poems ever composed.

> By the rivers of Babylon, there we sat down, yea, we wept, when we remembered Zion.
> We hanged our harps upon the willows in the midst thereof.
> For there they that carried us away captive required of us a song; and they that wasted us required of us mirth, saying, Sing us one of the songs of Zion.
> How shall we sing the Lord's song in a strange land?
>
> (Psalms 137:1–4)

After Nebuchadnezzar's death (562 B.C.), three ineffectual kings were succeeded by Nabonidus (555–539 B.C.), a peaceful, priestly scholar-king, whose son Belshazzar did the actual ruling. According to the famous Biblical story of the prophet Daniel, Belshazzar was at a banquet and, along with his court, was drinking from the golden vessels taken from the temple of Jerusalem, when a detached hand appeared, writing words on the wall: "Mene, mene, tekel, uphärsin." When no one was able to interpret the writing, Daniel was sent for, and the prophet read the words of doom for Babylon:

"God hath numbered thy kingdom, and finished it. . . . Thou art weighed in the balances, and art found wanting. . . . Thy kingdom is divided, and given to the Medes and Persians" (Daniel 5).

Daniel's words had a basis in fact. The Medes had been united with the Persians by Persia's King Cyrus (550–529 B.C.), a conqueror who found the rich lands of Babylonia too tempting to overlook. The scholarly Nabonidus and the desperate Belshazzar were no match for the fierce attacks of the Persians. But within the walls of Babylon, with provisions enough to withstand a siege of twenty years, Belshazzar could laugh at his enemies.

Cyrus was a clever man; according to tradition, he dug an enormous ditch around Babylon and diverted the Euphrates River from its normal course. This was done during one night, and his army was able to enter Babylon by marching up the old river bed that led into the city. Belshazzar and his household troops were killed, but Babylon was spared. The exiled Hebrews were permitted to return home, and the prophecy of Daniel was fulfilled.

A new era was opening in the ancient East. The Persians

and their successors, the Greeks and Romans, were rulers of an international world where commerce and industry were the reasons for cities and their growth. The day of the river-valley civilizations had passed, but Babylon the Great was always remembered as the last great glory of a culture that had lasted virtually intact for more than two thousand years.

# APPENDIX

❁ ❁ ❁ ❁ ❁ ❁ ❁ ❁ ❁ ❁ ❁ ❁

# GLOSSARY

❁ ❁ ❁ ❁ ❁ ❁ ❁ ❁ ❁ ❁ ❁ ❁

# SUGGESTIONS FOR FURTHER READING

❁ ❁ ❁ ❁ ❁ ❁ ❁ ❁ ❁ ❁ ❁ ❁

# INDEX

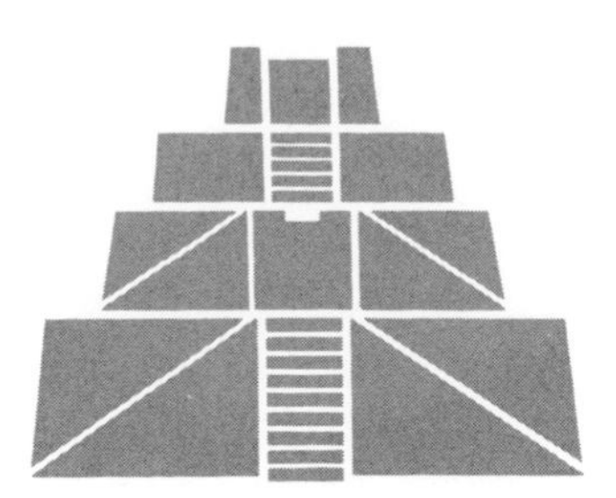

# APPENDIX

## A LISTING OF SOME DYNASTIES, KINGS, AND IMPORTANT DATES

2600–2050 B.C. Early Sumerian Dynasties
- Etana, the Shepherd King of Kish (hero of a myth; one of twenty-three kings whose reigns were said to total 24,500 years)
- Dumuzi the Fisherman, King of Erech
- Gilgamesh, King of Erech (hero of a myth; with Dumuzi, numbered among twelve kings whose reigns were said to total 23,000 years)

First Dynasty of Ur
- Mesannipadda
- Aannipadda
- Meskiagnanner
- Elulu
- Balulu

Lagash
- Urukagina
- Gudea

Third Dynasty of Erech
- Lugalzaggisi

2050–1960 B.C. Dynasty of Akkad
- Sargon I
- Naram-Sin

1960–1889 B.C. Third Dynasty of Ur (last great Sumerian dynasty)
- Ur-Nammu
- Shulgi
- Ibi-Sin

| | |
|---|---|
| 1800–1550 B.C. | First Dynasty of Babylon (Amorites) |
| | Hammurabi (ascended throne 1728 B.C.) |
| 1550–1170 B.C. | Kassites |
| 1170–883 B.C. | Gradual Rise of Assyrian Power |
| 883–626 B.C. | Rule of Assyrians |
| 883–859 B.C. | Assurnasirpal II |
| 858–824 B.C. | Shalmaneser III |
| 805–782 B.C. | Adadnirari III |
| 745–727 B.C. | Tiglathpileser III |
| 721–705 B.C. | Sargon II |
| 705–681 B.C. | Sennacherib |
| 680–669 B.C. | Esarhaddon |
| 668–626 B.C. | Assurbanipal |
| 612 B.C. | Fall of Nineveh |
| 612–539 B.C. | Neo-Babylonians (Chaldeans) |
| 625–605 B.C. | Nabopolassar |
| 604–562 B.C. | Nebuchadnezzar |
| 555–539 B.C. | Nabonidus and his son Belshazzar |
| 539 B.C. | Fall of Babylon |

# GLOSSARY

AKKADIANS. *A Semitic-language-speaking people who conquered Sumeria under Sargon around 2050* B.C. *Their capital was Babylon.*

AMORITES. *A Semitic people of the Arabian desert who frequently raided Sumeria.*

ANU (or AN). *The chief Sumerian god of heaven.*

ASHUR. *An important city in the south of Assyria. Also chief god of the Assyrians.*

CHALDEANS. *A Semitic people who settled in Babylonia around 1000* B.C. *They were families of the Neo-Babylonian empire* (ca. *612–539* B.C.). *Their most famous king was Nebuchadnezzar.*

CIVILIZATION. *A term meaning cities, or cultures influenced by cities, and their accomplishments. It is sometimes synonymous with urbanization.*

ELAMITES. *The name of an Iranian people living on the eastern borders of Sumeria.*

ENKI. *God of wisdom and creator of nature, including water.*

ENKIDU. *Friend of Gilgamesh in the epic.*

ENLIL. *God of the air. He is also known as the "father of the gods."*

ENSI. *Governor or ruler of a Sumerian city-state.*

ERECH. *The name of a city in southern Sumeria.*

ERIDU. *The name of a city in southern Sumeria.*

GILGAMESH. *King of Erech, hero of an epic account.*

GUTI. *A mountaineer people who lived to the east of Sumeria and often raided that land.*

ISHTAR. *Babylonian goddess of fertility. In Assyria she was regarded as the goddess of war.*

KASSITES. *A mountaineer people who invaded Babylonia around 1550* B.C. *They ruled until about 1100* B.C.

KHORSABAD. *Capital of Assyria during the reign of King Sargon II (721–705* B.C.*). The city was built by Sargon and is renowned for its palaces.*

KISH. *The name of a city in central Sumeria.*

LAGASH. *The name of a city in southern Sumeria.*

LARSA. *The name of a city in southern Sumeria.*

MALACHITE. *An ore of copper used in ancient times as a cure for eye disorders and as a cosmetic.*

MARDUK. *Chief god of the Babylonians.*

NANNA. *The moon god of the Sumerians.*

NIHMAH OR NINMAH OR NINHURSAG. *The Sumerian mother goddess from whom came all living things.*

NINEVEH. *An important city in central Assyria.*

NINGAL. *Wife of the moon god Sin.*

SHINAR. *The great alluvial plain to the south of Babylon, extending to the Persian Gulf. This was the seat of ancient Sumeria.*

SHURUPPAK. *A Sumerian city.*

SIN. *Moon god of the Sumerians.*

TIAMAT. *Goddess of the chaos. She is depicted as a dragon.*

UR. *The name of a city in southern Sumeria.*

UTNAPISHTIM. *A mortal who had received the gift of eternal life in the Gilgamesh epic.*

WEIR. *A kind of dam or diversionary construction to force water into a canal.*

ZIGGURAT. *A platform built in stages and on which was situated a temple. The temple was reached by stairways and/or ramps.*

# SUGGESTIONS FOR FURTHER READING

CAMERON, G. G., *The Comparative Stratigraphy of Early Iran,* Chicago, University of Chicago Press, 1942.

CHIERA, EDWARD, *They Wrote on Clay* (2nd ed.), Chicago, Phoenix Books, University of Chicago Press, 1955.

FINEGAN, J., *Light from the Ancient Past,* Princeton, N.J., Princeton University Press, 1949.

FRANKFORT, H., *The Art and Architecture of the Ancient Orient,* Harmondsworth, England, Penguin Books, 1959.

FRANKFORT, H. (ed.), *Before Philosophy,* Harmondsworth, England, Penguin Books, 1959.

GHIRSHMAN, R., *Iran,* Harmondsworth, England, Penguin Books, 1954.

HERZFELD, E., *Archaeological History of Iran,* London, Oxford University Press, 1935.

HOOKS, S. H., *Babylonian and Assyrian Religion,* Norman, Okla., University of Oklahoma Press, 1963.

KRAMER, SAMUEL N., *From the Tablets of Sumer,* Indian Hills, Colo., Falcon's Wing Press, 1956.

KRAMER, SAMUEL N., *Sumerian Mythology,* New York, Harper & Row, 1961.

KRAMER, SAMUEL N., *The Sumerians,* Chicago, University of Chicago Press, 1963.

LLOYD, SETON, *Twin Rivers* (2nd ed.), London, Oxford University Press, 1947.

LLOYD, SETON, *Foundations in the Dust,* Harmondsworth, England, Penguin Books, 1955.

OLMSTEAD, A. T., *A History of Assyria,* New York, Charles Scribner's Sons, 1924.

OLMSTEAD, A. T., *History of the Persian Empire,* Chicago, Phoenix Books, University of Chicago Press, 1959.

PERKINS, ANN L., *The Comparative Archaeology of Early Mesopotamia,* Chicago, University of Chicago Press, 1949.

PRITCHARD, J. B. (ed.), *Ancient Near Eastern Texts,* Princeton, N.J., Princeton University Press, 1955.

WOOLLEY, C. LEONARD, *Ur of the Chaldeans,* Harmondsworth, England, Penguin Books, 1952.

WOOLLEY, C. LEONARD, *Excavations at Ur,* London, Ernest Benn, 1954.

WOOLLEY, C. LEONARD, *The Art of the Middle East,* New York, Crown Publishers, 1961.

# INDEX

Figures in **boldface** type indicate pages with pictures.

# ABOUT THE AUTHOR

WALTER A. FAIRSERVIS, JR., is Associate Professor in Anthropology at the University of Washington and Director of the Thomas Burke Memorial Washington State Museum of the University of Washington in Seattle; he is also a Research Associate in the Department of Anthropology of the American Museum of Natural History in New York City. Dr. Fairservis has participated in numerous archaeological expeditions in the Middle and Far East and in Egypt. He has also traveled widely in Europe and Africa.

He is the author of a number of books, among them *Egypt, Gift of the Nile* in this series; he has written many archaeological reports and is a frequent contributor to scientific journals.

Dr. Fairservis was born in New York City; he and his wife Jan—an illustrator who supplied the drawings used in this volume—and their three daughters now live in Seattle, Washington.